D0970563

EVERYTHING CHANGES

WHEN YOU SEE GOD FOR WHO HE REALLY IS

GOD
IS
AMAZING

BRUCE BICKEL
STAN JANTZ

SHILOH RUN  PRESS
An Imprint of Barbour Publishing, Inc.

*Our mission is to publish and distribute inspirational products offering exceptional
value and biblical encouragement to the masses.*

Member of the
Evangelical Christian
Publishers Association

Contents

Introduction

Our world is an amazing place. But most people are either too focused on "important" things or with truly trivial matters to notice.

We understand that. When you're rushing around the house trying to get the kids off to school or running late for work because you're stuck in traffic, you don't consider the amazing fact that once again, for the umpteenth time, a massive ball of hot plasma 93 million miles away is warming our planet so we can live another day.

It's only natural to take nature for granted. But every once in a while we should stop and smell the roses. We should notice the astonishing wonders of the natural world. Even more, we should lift our eyes beyond the natural to the supernatural—to our amazing God, who created it all. He is the One who gives us life and breath and everything else.

Twenty centuries ago on the Sea of Galilee, a

body of water in what is now Israel, twelve ordinary men were in a boat. A great storm arose, and the boat was swamped. The men panicked and sought their leader—who was sleeping while the storm raged. "Save us, Lord," they cried. "We are going to die." Their leader got up, said "Peace! Be still," and instantly the wind and the waves calmed. The men were amazed and afraid—not at the miracle they had just witnessed, but at the supernatural being in their presence. "Who is this, that even the wind and the sea obey Him?" they whispered. The man, of course, was Jesus Christ, God in human form, who amazed people throughout His earthly existence by the things He did and the life He lived.

Like the men in that boat, we are too often focused on the circumstances around us, whether extraordinary or routine. We often fail to notice the amazing God who's right there with us. When the sea is calm, we take Him for granted. When the storm is raging, we forget He's near.

How tragic! No matter what we're going through, no matter how ordinary or how challenging life may be, we need to think about God first, realizing with every ounce of our being that God is amazing. Everything about Him—from His amazing power to His amazing grace—is absolutely real, not the stuff of myth or conjecture. He is as real as the beautiful world He made. He is more amazing than we could ever imagine.

In this book we want to encourage you to know

and more fully appreciate your amazing God. We will consider Him from four different perspectives:

- In Part 1, we consider the amazing characteristics of God's being.
- In Part 2, we look at the world God made and show how its wonders point to His wonders.
- The theme of Part 3 is Jesus, who astonished the world with His love and sacrifice—and continues to amaze us today.
- Finally, in Part 4, we show how God's amazing grace is lived out every day in people just like you.

It's time for a bigger view of God. We hope you're ready to lift your eyes and begin to truly appreciate Him. And, in doing so, that you'll truly love Him with all your heart, soul, mind, and strength.

PART I

AMAZING GOD

INTRODUCTION

People are often befuddled when it comes to discussing the nature of God. We know how to describe most animate and inanimate items in our lives, but God seems to transcend the usual descriptive lingo we find convenient and informative when discussing other subjects.

Usually, the answers to a few standard questions can draw out all we care to know about a person or thing, whether that's an exotic automobile, the next-generation mobile computing device, or your best friend: What does it do? What does it look like? How can it benefit me? But such a simple line of inquiry is insufficient when considering an amazing God who is both infinite and mysterious. A simple question-and-answer checklist is woefully inadequate to offer an understanding of the incomprehensible.

Theologians—who are paid to know things about God—often defer to a descriptive list of His *attributes*.

But that seems to us a rather clinical and impersonal approach. This is not how people describe someone they find fascinating or captivating. Imagine a local television news reporter interviewing the groom during a wedding reception and asking a penetrating line of questions:

"Why have you picked *this* woman to be your bride?"

"What do you find so fascinating about her?"

"What makes her character and personality so irresistible to you?"

"What do you find most attractive about her?"

You can be sure this interview wouldn't make the evening broadcast if the groom replies with a dispassionate, "Let me list for you her attributes, all of which I find admirable."

That kind of parlance may be acceptable in seminary classrooms, but it is not how regular people describe someone with whom they are captivated.

We (the authors of this book) find God amazing. And, like a lot of other people, we can't shut up about Him. We can't help becoming enthused when we describe Him to other people. Later in this book, we'll focus on the answers to the "What Does He Do?" and the "How Can He Benefit You?" questions. But in Part 1, we'd like to hone in on twelve aspects of His personality, character, and nature—all of which are unique to Him in that no other being in the universe possesses them.

If you want to sound spiritual and studious, you can refer to these distinctives as "attributes." We simply prefer to think of them as the aspects of God that blow us away.

CHAPTER 1

....

GOD IS SELF-SUFFICIENT

*"The God who made the world and everything in it is
the Lord of heaven and earth and does not live in
temples built by human hands. And he is not served
by human hands, as if he needed anything. Rather,
he himself gives everyone life and breath and everything else."*

THE APOSTLE PAUL

ACTS 17:24–25

One of the most amazing things about God—His
self-sufficiency—is also one of the hardest to comprehend. It's not very difficult to think of God being
so powerful that He could create the universe. Even
people who don't think much about God can at least
imagine how an almighty higher power could bring
the world into existence. But the idea that God is
uncreated and completely self-sufficient, that He has

no beginning and has always existed with no help from any other power—well, that just isn't comprehensible to our finite human minds.

The self-existence of God is such a primal puzzlement that even a child, when told that God made the world, will often respond with the question, "Who made God?" This remarkable bit of reasoning shows that children understand the concept of cause and effect: if something or someone exists, then something or someone else had to have made it.

It's as if the human race has an origin-seeking gene. We want to know where things came from and how stuff happened. We're like the police interrogator who asks a suspect, "Where were you on the night of August 27?" because he is following the scientific task of accounting for things and being skeptical of anything that hasn't given an account for itself.

One of the reasons so many people are skeptical about God is that He *won't* give an account of Himself. We want to know where He came from, but He won't tell us. Instead, He just reveals to us that He is and always was, and with no outside help. God doesn't fit into our cause-and-effect world, and that frustrates us to no end.

Thank God He doesn't exist within the bounds of cause and effect. If God were the effect of some other cause, He wouldn't be God and we wouldn't exist. You see, you can't have an endless series of causes reaching back into eternity past. If that were the case, you would never get to the present time, and you would never get to *you*. The very fact that you and the world exist is proof that at some point there must be a First Cause that itself isn't caused. There must be an originator. There must be God.

Is your mind spinning yet? Hang on, because here is where it gets really amazing. Take all the wonder of the world and the history of humanity—the billions and billions of people who have ever lived and everything they have accomplished. None of them would have existed were it not for God.

Set aside the *proofs* for the existence of God and ponder this single startling reality: if there is no God, there's nothing else. But there *is* something. There's you and your life and your ability to think about a self-sufficient God who doesn't *need* you for His existence because He was here way before you. And yet He *wants* you to realize He exists so that you can experience His goodness, grace, and love.

God doesn't need us, but He wants us to enjoy Him. Why do you think God didn't just make a world with nothing but dull features but instead created extravagant beauty and unimaginable variety? The simplest and best answer is that He created it all for our enjoyment. He wants us to see the world and everything in it and then give Him the credit for getting it all going.

Two thousand years ago the apostle Paul was walking through Athens, a great city filled with smart and religious people who preferred to give credit to man-made idols rather than the living God. Paul boldly told them that God was the One "who made the world and everything in it, being Lord of heaven and earth." Furthermore, Paul continued, He is not "served by human hands, as though he needed anything, since he himself gives to all mankind breath and everything" (Acts 17:24–25 ESV).

Some of the Athenians got it, but many didn't—much like it is with people today. So don't get discouraged if others don't share your amazement at the First-Cause God. They're looking for answers in man-made objects. Keep your eyes and your heart and your mind focused on the One who made everything possible.

CHAPTER 2

....

GOD IS INVISIBLE AND SPIRITUAL

*To say that God is invisible is to walk
around with your eyes closed.*
ANDREW PETERSON

The power of invisibility is cool if you are a superhero, but it can have some disadvantages if you are a supreme being. For example, skeptics assert that God does not exist because we cannot see Him. But the fact of God's invisibility does not limit His ability to make Himself known, nor does it inhibit His power to reveal His strength and His presence.

The Bible describes God as invisible with statements such as: "No one has ever seen God" (John 1:18) and "Now to the King eternal, immortal, invisible, the only God, be honor and glory for ever and ever" (1 Timothy 1:17). Because humans don't have much experience with invisibility, we tend to think that anything we can't see doesn't have much substance. After all, our thoughts are invisible, but they vanish at the slightest distraction, perhaps never to be recaptured. But being invisible doesn't imply that God is a wispy, ethereal essence without substance. Like a violent wind, you might not see Him approaching, but He can make His presence known.

But don't let God's invisibility fool you. He is there—just not usually in a physical form, for the Bible also describes Him as being a Spirit. As Jesus said: "God is spirit, and those who worship him must worship in spirit and truth" (John 4:24 ESV). He is invisible *because* He is a spirit and not flesh. So God has no form, no physical body. The absence of a physical body could be a disadvantage to a human, but being a form-free spirit facilitates other awesome characteristics that are unique to God—such as being unrestricted by the space-and-time continuum in which humanity operates.

Rather than being a handicap to proving God's existence, the invisible and spirit nature of God allows Him creativity and impact whenever and however He chooses to reveal Himself to earth's inhabitants. The bottom line is this: if God were limited to human form, He wouldn't be any more spectacular. But as an invisible spirit, He has the ability to present Himself through attention-grabbing modalities:

- In some manner, God appeared to Adam in

the Garden of Eden. Adam and Eve "heard the sound of LORD God walking in the garden in the cool of the day" (Genesis 3:8 ESV).

- God and two angels appeared as sojourners to Abraham, who invited them to dinner around a campfire (see Genesis 18:2–5).
- God appeared and spoke to Moses from a burning bush (see Exodus 3).
- When the Israelites wandered in the wilderness for forty years, God showed up as a pillar of clouds in the daytime and as a pillar of fire in the evening (see Exodus 13:21–22).

While an enflamed shrub or a cloud column are impressive, these phenomena don't particularly project a personal, relational God. Yet God is all about a personal and intimate relationship with the members of the human race. So, through His supernatural capabilities, He is able to connect with us as a loving Father, despite being invisible and without form. Although He has no physical body, the Bible attributes to God anthropomorphic characteristics than help us envision how He can care for, protect, and love us. Thus, the Scripture tells us that:

- God's *eyes* are on us (Psalm 33:18)
- If we ask anything according to His will, He *hears* us (1 John 5:15)
- The righteous are in God's *hands* (Ecclesiastes 9:1)
- God *speaks* to us (Psalm 85:8)

In addition to these physical similarities to us, the invisible God who is without form or body expresses emotions to which every human can relate. He experiences and expresses anger, laughter, compassion, grief, jealousy, wrath, joy, and love. While He may be invisible and a spirit, He knows our human emotions and shares them with us. He has experienced suffering, and He can offer understanding and comfort to us in the midst of ours.

Knowing that humans are dense when it comes to spiritual matters, God knew that we needed something much more obvious than an invisible God. So, through a supernatural transformation, God assumed human form and established residency on earth for approximately thirty-three years. In the God-Man of Jesus Christ, the human race was exposed to God in the flesh. And there was no beating around a burning bush about this. He proclaimed it clearly as the Son of God: "Anyone who has seen me has seen the Father" (John 14:9). Jesus wasn't referring to His facial features or His physique. Rather, He was saying that His character, His teaching, and His actions were accurate reflections of His heavenly Father.

How awesome is that? This invisible God of ours went to great lengths to make His existence obvious and to make His nature known to all of us.

CHAPTER 3

....

GOD IS ETERNAL, INFINITE, AND EVERYWHERE

From everlasting to everlasting you are God.
MOSES
PSALM 90:2

Many things about our amazing God are difficult for our finite minds to grasp, but the most challenging may be the idea that He is eternal, infinite, and everywhere. We can understand and even relate to other aspects of His being—His love, His grace, His power—but His eternity, infinity, and omnipresence seem beyond our comprehension, mainly because we have no point of reference.

It's hard for us to think about eternity because there's nothing in our experience to measure it against. We try to come up with clever analogies, such as the parable of a little bird that goes to a huge mountain once every thousand years to sharpen its beak. When the mountain has been worn away by this periodic beak sharpening, a single day of eternity will have passed. Cute story, but even that fails to capture the true essence of eternity because it describes an activity that is bound by time. Truthfully, there's nothing we can use to describe eternity or even compare it to because there's only one being who is truly eternal, and that's our indescribable, incomparable, amazing God.

While *eternity* has to do with His existence, *infinity* describes His being. To say God is eternal is to say He has no beginning and no end. Since God is self-existent and uncreated, He exists outside of time. By comparison, the *infinite* part of God's being means that everything about God—His love, His grace, His power—knows no bounds. And all of that infinitude belongs to you. What this means for you is intensely personal and practical. Your needs, no matter how great, will never exhaust the infinite resources of God.

God's *eternal* existence and *infinite* being are complemented by the reality that He is *everywhere*. Or to use theological language, God is *omnipresent*. On the face of it, this makes God sound abstract and distant. In fact, the word has a very different meaning. As A. W. Tozer points out, "the word *present* means here, close to, next to, and the prefix *omni* gives it universality." So to say that God is omnipresent is to mean that He is right there close to you—no matter who you are or where you are.

The French mystic Hildebert of Lavardin described God's omnipresence like this:

God is over all things, under all things; outside all;
within but not enclosed; without but not excluded;
above but not raised up; below but not depressed;
wholly above, presiding, wholly beneath,
sustaining; wholly within, filling.

Such a lofty concept is almost too amazing for us to comprehend. Part of the difficulty lies in our attachment to our material universe. Even those who believe in God can live day-to-day as if there's nothing beyond what they can touch, taste, feel, or see. With such a practical and natural mind-set, it's a struggle to imagine a supernatural God who is everywhere yet always somewhere. But the Bible teaches and Christians believe that the world is essentially spiritual. It was created out of nothing by a God who is Spirit, and though the material aspect of our universe is all around us in the form of matter, it's the unseen reality—the spiritual essence of the world—that really matters. For here is where the eternal, infinite, omnipresent God dwells. He created time and material for us, but He cannot be contained by either one.

God's grandeur would be difficult to grasp were it not for His omnipresence. Because of this quality, God is both near us and in us by way of His Spirit. He always sees us, not to find fault and punish us, but to know and bless us. The presence of God in our lives is unlike any other experience. In this way God is a source of pleasure in the midst of our pain. He is our sustainer no matter where we are.

As fragile, finite beings who have experienced our share of difficulty and tragedy, God's eternal being, infinite nature, and omnipresence are within our grasp because God is personal. God is bigger and more amazing than we can imagine yet more approachable than we could ever dream. This isn't a fantasy. This is real because God is real. He knows exactly who He is, and He longs for you to know Him just as He is.

"I am God, and there is no other; I am God, and there is none like me. I make known the end from the beginning, from ancient times, what is still to come."
ISAIAH 46:9–10

CHAPTER 4

GOD IS UNCHANGING

"I the LORD do not change."
MALACHI 3:6

There is a growing belief among many Christians today that God, in order to keep up with our changing culture, is evolving. People in the past didn't know God the way we do, this line of thinking goes, so their ideas of God were incomplete. Today, we know better, and God "understands," so what was once considered wrong or taboo is now true and acceptable. He's a pragmatic God, after all, and He doesn't want His followers to embarrass themselves in a culture that is more "tolerant" than past cultures were.

As popular as this notion is these days, we urge you not to buy into it—mainly because it shows a misunderstanding of the character of our amazing

God. As you are discovering as you read this book (and perhaps already knew), every aspect of God's personality is important. No one of God's qualities should be magnified so that it overshadows the others, and none can be minimized for our convenience.

One of those traits often minimized or overlooked is God's immutability, which is another way of saying God doesn't change. We sometimes struggle with this one, because we view change as good. The poet E.E. Cummings wrote, "It takes courage to grow up and become who you truly are." We don't disagree with that, as long as you're applying it to us mortals. We humans need to change so we can reach our full potential, whether it's physically, mentally, or spiritually. That's fine for us, because we can always do better. But God doesn't need to do better. He doesn't need to reach His full potential, and He doesn't need to become more than He is. God cannot become *more* eternal, *more* infinite, *more* powerful, or *more* holy. He is at the apex of all those qualities. He is as perfect and fully realized as He can be.

God certainly doesn't need to change His character to accommodate a shift in our culture. He is the North Star, fixed in position while everything else changes. His character and actions are utterly reliable. You can always count on Him to be faithful and true. Nothing that happens in our world takes Him by surprise, so He never needs to make an adjustment. There are no contingencies to the things that have or could happen that God has not already taken into consideration.

God is our "refuge and strength, a very present help in trouble" (Psalm 46:1 ESV).

God's unchanging nature also means He will not respond to our deficiencies with anything that denies His character. At the end of his ministry, just before his life was ended at the hands of Roman executioners, the apostle Paul wrote: "If we are faithless, he remains faithful—for he cannot deny himself" (2 Timothy 2:13 ESV). Clearly, Paul understood that despite our trials and our unfaithfulness—and both are going to happen at points in our lives—God does not change. He remains our rock and our fortress. What an amazing reality!

But what about those cases when God seems to change His mind? A few times in the Bible, God threatened to punish people, but then "changed His mind" when someone (such as Abraham, Moses, or Jonah) pleaded and asked Him to reconsider. In these cases, the Scriptures tell us that God "relented" (see Exodus 32:14; Jonah 3:10). Does that mean He changed by changing His mind?

It's tempting to "anthropomorphize" God—that is, make Him human—but that's not the right approach. Rather than bringing God to our level, we need to lift our eyes and appreciate our amazing God for who He really is, even if it's difficult to comprehend.

What seems like change to us is just God being God. As Michael Horton says, "He is so active and dynamic that no change can make Him more active."

You see, *immutability* does not mean *immobility*.

God is incredibly active in the world. He's constantly creating, sustaining, and redeeming. Because of His inexhaustible depth of wisdom and knowledge (see Romans 11:33), His works are always generative, generous, and gratuitous—and He does this all for you!

At the end of every day, as you reflect on all that happened as you thought about God, talked about God, and talked with God, you should have a deep sense of peace and assurance as you realize that God will never change in His love for you and will never diminish in His desire or ability to help you. God will always be what He has always been. Nothing more and nothing less.

CHAPTER 5

....

GOD IS LOVING

God is love. He didn't need us. But he wanted us.
And that is the most amazing thing.
RICK WARREN

Don't take our word for it. Hear it from the apostle John, the guy who was perhaps Christ's closest earthly friend. He described God with this amazingly straightforward statement: "God is love" (1 John 4:8). You can't get much more succinct than that.

This is not a new concept for most people. We've seen the bumper stickers and heard the sermons. Maybe we're so overexposed to the foundational truth that "God is love" that most of us have become immune to its incredible impact. To make matters worse, we live in a culture that has devalued the ideal of love. It has been removed from the realm of the divine and lowered to the level of human amorousness. Our culture is inundated with an emphasis on romance, with contestants vying to win the affection of a bachelor or bachelorette, with websites devoted to making connections between persons looking for love, and Twitter followers monitoring the love-lives of celebrities. All of this reinforces a human context for love that pales in comparison to the amazing characteristics of God's love.

God's love stands in sharp contrast to human notions of love. For us, love is predicated on feelings and affected by emotions. It's mercurial and can change from one moment to the next. That's why people can easily "fall in" or "fall out of" love. Although we may have intense affection for someone, at its core this kind of love is based on a foundation of conditionality. We love someone as long as we receive a reciprocal benefit. We must be loved in return. And this is where God's love stands in stark contrast to human love.

Amazingly, God's love is all about commitment. In the New Testament, the Greek word used to describe God's love is *agape*. It connotes the deepest, purest kind of love—a love that is not based on emotions but results as an act of one's will. It is intentional. Equating love with commitment gives deeper meaning to familiar verses:

- "For God [was so committed to] the world that he gave his one and only Son, that whoever believes in him shall not perish but have eternal life" (John 3:16).

- "This is how God showed his [commitment] among us: He sent his one and only Son into the world that we might live through him" (1 John 4:9).

This means that God's love is unconditional. When love extends based on commitment, it is given because of the character of the person doing the loving and not because of the worthiness of the object of the love. God doesn't love us because we are loveable or because we make Him feel good. (What a relief! Our track record in that regard is not stellar.) Simply, He loves just because He *is* love.

Unconditional love takes all the pressure off us. We don't need to live in fear that we might offend God and lose His love. Certainly, we will fail and lapse into disobedience, but just as certainly, God's love will persist because it is not based on our performance but on His character.

The story of the Prodigal Son from Luke 15 illustrates this principle. A rebellious son leaves his loving father's home, taking his inheritance in advance. He blows his fortune in an excessive and indulgent lifestyle. When he hits rock bottom, he has nowhere to turn but back to the father he had so cavalierly disrespected and rejected. Amazingly, the father welcomes his son back into the family—demanding no apology or punishment—and celebrates the restoration of their relationship. Through the entire ordeal, the father's love was unabated and unaltered by the son's offenses.

God's love is also distinguished from human love by its sacrificial qualities. Human love tends to be self-centered, always mindful of how we are being treated in return. It is just the opposite with God's love. His love is sacrificial. There is no self-interest, even to the point of death: "This is how we know what [God's] love is: Jesus Christ laid down his life for us" (1 John 3:16).

God's love is divine, not only in the sense of being unconditional, but also in the respect that He enables us to replicate His love to others. He does not keep His love within His own domain but infuses it into our lives so that we might extend it to others. That enables us to be God's emissaries, those who have been given the supernatural ability to love like Jesus.

There's nothing mundane about that kind of love. There is nothing human about it, either. And that's what makes it so amazing.

CHAPTER 6

GOD IS JUST AND RIGHTEOUS

God is not defined by the term "righteous" as much as the term "righteous" is defined by God. God is not measured by the standard of righteousness; God sets the standard of righteousness.
BOB DEFFINBAUGH

While the New Testament tends to more prominently emphasize God's love, the righteousness and justice of God grabs most of the headlines in the Old Testament.

It is easy to understand why people gravitate toward the love side of God, while paying less attention to the fact that He is a righteous and just God. We tend to enjoy God's love but want to avoid thinking about His judgment.

Actually, we want a God who is fair and just when dealing with people who have done us wrong; we just don't want a God with such high standards sitting in judgment over ourselves. But understanding God isn't like assembling a Mr. Potato Head; we don't get to pick and choose the traits we like and leave the others in a box.

The righteousness of God is virtually synonymous with His justice. If there is a distinction, we usually think of God's righteousness in reference to His thoughts and actions, and His justice in terms of how He administers judgment. But underlying both terms is the truth that God always does what is right. He is fair and impartial. He doesn't play favorites and shows no partiality. These are divine qualities, and they are deservedly praised in scripture:

- "He is the Rock, his works are perfect, and all his ways are just. A faithful God who does no wrong, upright and just is he" (Deuteronomy 32:4).
- "Your righteousness is like the highest mountains, your justice like the great deep" (Psalm 36:6).
- "And the heavens proclaim his righteousness, for he is a God of justice" (Psalm 50:6).
- "But the LORD Almighty will be exalted by his justice, and the holy God will be proved holy by his righteous acts" (Isaiah 5:16).

God's righteousness is not determined according to some behavioral checklist or universal criteria. *He* is the standard *because* He is righteous. That would sound like a self-serving argument if we were talking about ourselves. But this is God we're talking about, and He is wholly holy. (Skip to ahead to Chapter 12 if this concept is gnawing at you.)

We can take comfort in a God of justice and righteousness. From a cosmic perspective, you can be confident that evil will eventually be conquered and eternally exterminated. On a more personal level, when you are suffering because of unfair treatment and injustice, you can be assured that God's justice will ultimately prevail. You can trust the conclusion of these matters to Him because He is righteous and just.

But the prospect of facing an eternal judge who is wholly righteous is unnerving. Most of us would prefer a judge who has blundered through life—just like we have—and has a list of major screw-ups in his life. We don't want someone who has always abided by "doing the right thing." But God's righteousness (remember, He *always* does the right thing) prohibits Him from cutting us any slack, or letting us off easy. Our sinfulness deserves a penalty. According to scripture, we have all sinned (Romans 3:23) and the penalty for our sins is death (Romans 6:23).

But fear not. Our amazing God has a plan that exonerates us without violating His righteousness or divine sense of justice. We aren't just "let off the hook," or just declared "not guilty." It goes deeper than that, as God determines us to be righteous. How's that for a plot twist? Here's how it works: Christ—who was perfect and never did evil, and was therefore not deserving of any punishment—took on the sins of all humanity and the concomitant death penalty. He died in our place so that we could be reconciled with God and be declared completely righteous. Theologian R.C. Sproul gives this summary:

> *When a person becomes a Christian and has authentic faith, he has a real mystical union with Christ, so that Christ really comes to indwell the believer. When we exercise faith in Jesus Christ, His righteousness is counted towards us and we are justified. At that same moment, Christ, by virtue of the Holy Spirit, comes to dwell inside of us.*

To be "justified" is far better than merely being declared "not guilty." Being justified means that we are righteous before God. When we align ourselves with Christ, God imputes Christ's righteous to us, just as He charged the guilt of our sins to His Son.

Not only do we have a God who is absolutely and completely righteous, but He has also made a way (at the cost of His Son's sacrificial death) for *us* to become righteous as well. The amazing result is that we, being sinful, can now enjoy the privilege of being considered His children for all eternity.

CHAPTER 7

....

GOD IS MERCIFUL AND GRACIOUS

*"The LORD, the LORD, the compassionate and gracious God,
slow to anger, abounding in love and faithfulness."*
EXODUS 34:6

We humans usually have a pretty high opinion of ourselves. Generally speaking, we don't struggle with confidence and self-esteem. And that's a good thing; in fact, it's a God-given thing. God has made humans with the unique abilities to dream and aspire, to conceive and achieve, to explore and create. These qualities are the reason we have discovered new worlds, developed cures for diseases, written great literature, composed beautiful music, and turned ones and zeroes into machines capable of astounding computations.

Of course, these virtuous human abilities have led to one of humanity's greatest vices: pride. We are proud of what we can and have accomplished—to the point where we doubt that there's anything we can't do.

Pride can be inspiring and beautiful, such as when a citizen is proud of his country or a parent is proud of her child. But when pride leads to arrogance, it makes us ugly. The famous Tower of Babel in the Old Testament is symbolic of our tendency to want to "make a name for ourselves" and be self-sufficient apart from God (see Genesis 11:1–9). More often than not, pride gets us into trouble because it prevents us from accepting the help we desperately need. It's the reason for the famous proverb, "Pride goes before destruction, a haughty spirit before a fall" (Proverbs 16:18).

Pride leads to our downfall most quickly when we reject God's grace. When you think about it, this is an astounding reality of the human condition. God's amazing grace is the most beautiful and life-giving gift He could ever offer, yet the vast majority of people living in the world made by His gracious hand are too proud to accept it. We think we can *earn* God's favor because we have achieved great things. We fail to realize that we are poor and pitiful in and of ourselves, that there's nothing we can offer God in terms of performance or achievement.

This isn't a popular idea in this era, when we place so much importance on self-esteem, but it's true. We humans are, by and large, a nasty bunch. That's not to say that every person is as bad as he or she could be. But if we're honest with ourselves, we would have to admit that there's something in the human condition that keeps us from being as good as we could be.

By God's standard, which is perfection (see the chapter on God's holiness), we have missed the mark. In fact, that's the definition of sin—and there's not one person who lives now or who has ever lived (other than Jesus Christ) who hasn't fallen short of God's perfect standard. But rather than condemn us, which God has every right to do, He gives us grace. That's not based on anything we have done but according to His generous favor.

J. I. Packer uses these eloquent words to describe the essence of God's grace:

> *The grace of God is love freely shown towards guilty sinners, contrary to their merit and indeed in defiance of their demerit. It is God showing goodness to persons who deserve only severity, and had no reason to expect anything but severity.*

The result of God's grace—freely given and gratefully received by us—is salvation, a word prideful people don't like to talk about. And why should they? Only a person who's drowning needs to be saved. But isn't that the point? We're *all* drowning; we just don't know it. We're all in need of salvation, even if we don't recognize it. You may be perfectly fine living as a self-sufficient human being, but you are surrounded on all sides by human misery, most of it inflicted by other humans. And in your own heart, you know that you're just as guilty of hurting others as anyone can be.

A. W. Tozer observes this about grace and mercy: If grace is God's goodness offered to offensive and guilty human beings, then mercy is God's goodness confronting human misery and guilt. Grace is what God gives to undeserving people, while mercy is what He *doesn't* give to deserving people. We deserve judgment, but God freely pardons us, if only we will accept what He freely offers.

The amazing thing about God is that He doesn't ask us to pass any tests. He doesn't require a 100 percent on the final. All He asks is that we believe and receive:

"For God so loved the world that he gave his one and only Son, that whoever believes in him shall not perish but have eternal life."
JOHN 3:16

CHAPTER 8

....

GOD IS ALL-KNOWING AND ALL-WISE

*To say that God is omniscient is to say that
He possesses perfect knowledge and therefore has
no need to learn. But it is more: it is to say that
God has never learned and cannot learn.*

A.W. TOZER

The term *know-it-all* is usually used in a derogatory and sarcastic sense. But with God, it is a true statement for which He is worthy of high praise. God is the only one who possesses limitless knowledge. That isn't an exaggeration in any respect, for there is nothing He does not know. The theological term for this attribute of God is *omniscience*, as in "God is omniscient."

We're talking about much more here than a masterful grasp on trivia. (Although according to Matthew

10:30, He knows the number of hairs on your head.) The breadth of His knowledge encompasses everything you would want your Supreme Being to be aware of. When the Bible says that God knows everything (see 1 John 3:20), we can understand why—but only if we know a little something about the true nature of God. He knows everything that has happened in the past because He existed before time began. And He knows every present occurrence because He is everywhere, all at the same time, so nothing happens outside His view. But some aspects of His omniscience—and their impact—are not so obvious:

- *God knows the future*: "I am God, and there is no other; I am God, and there is none like me, declaring the end from the beginning and from ancient times things not yet done. . ." (Isaiah 46:9–10 esv). There is no "Plan B" with God, and nothing ever catches Him by surprise. Events in your life may take you by surprise, but you'll never hear God say: "Wow! I didn't see that one coming." So you can choose to live by your own plan and risk the consequences. Or you can choose to follow the plan of the One who knows the results in advance.
- *God knows every thought*: ". . . acknowledge the God of your father, and serve him with wholehearted devotion and with a willing mind, for the LORD searches every heart and

understands every desire and every thought" (1 Chronicles 28:9). God knows what you are thinking, even when you don't utter a word. This is why Jesus could speak so confidently when He chided religious leaders of His time for their hypocrisy. (This should encourage you to be honest with the Lord. He knows what's in your heart and mind, so pretending won't fool Him.)

- *God knows every human need*: ". . .your Father knows what you need before you ask him" (Matthew 6:8). You may not even know what you really need, but God does. This can come in handy when our prayers are off-target. Thankfully, He may not give us what we ask for but rather bestows on us what He knows we need.

Perhaps you've heard the expression "knowledge is power." That's not exactly true—at least not for us humans. History has not shown that the winning contestants on television's *Jeopardy!* are particularly powerful. It isn't knowledge of facts that makes one powerful; it is the effective application of that knowledge in present circumstances. And that combination—knowledge plus judgment—is referred to as *wisdom*.

It shouldn't surprise you to know that God, the One who is all-knowing, is also all-wise: "To God belong wisdom and power; counsel and understanding are his" (Job 12:13). Trusting God is easier for us when we realize that He knows what is best for us. He knows our strengths and weaknesses, our fears and desires; He knows the circumstances that surround us now, and those we will face in the future. He loves us, wants what is best for us, and has the wisdom to know the best course of action for our circumstances.

Because God is sovereign and controls the events in our lives, He can bring about good even when the outlook is bleak. The apostle Paul put it this way: "And we know that in all things God works for the good of those who love him, who have been called according to his purpose" (Romans 8:28).

God's knowledge and wisdom are so amazing that you won't always be able to figure out what He is doing in your life. Sometimes, you might even think that He doesn't know what He is doing. But He does. He has the credentials, so you can trust Him even though you don't understand what He is doing. You can trust Him when He says:

"For my thoughts are not your thoughts, neither are your ways my ways," declares the LORD. "As the heavens are higher than the earth, so are my ways higher than your ways and my thoughts than your thoughts."
ISAIAH 55:8–9

CHAPTER 9

GOD IS FAITHFUL

*"Know therefore that the LORD your God is God,
the faithful God who keeps covenant and steadfast love
with those who love him and keep his commandments,
to a thousand generations."*
DEUTERONOMY 7:9 ESV

Lose fifteen pounds in fifteen days without dieting or exercise! Become a millionaire by building your own website. No knowledge of computers necessary!

Such promises sound too good to be true, and most of us instinctively know they can't be trusted. A promise is only good when it is kept. *Making* the promise is easy, and anyone can do it. But *keeping* the promise requires faithfulness on the part of the one who has made it.

There are a lot of con artists out there making

promises they have no intention of keeping. God isn't one of them. The Bible describes Him as a "faithful" God. This means that His words are true and that He keeps His promises. The prophet Jeremiah wrote of this quality of God, "The steadfast love of the Lord never ceases; his mercies never come to an end; they are new every morning; great is your faithfulness" (Lamentations 3:22–23 ESV).

God has made lots of promises. In the Old Testament, He made—and kept—promises to Noah, Abraham, Moses, and others. But let's get a little more "up close and personal" with this issue: God has made promises to *you*. Here are just a few of them:

- If you confess your sins, He will forgive your sins and cleanse you from all unrighteousness (see 1 John 1:9).
- God will supply all your needs (see Philippians 4:19).
- God will give you eternal life if you become a follower of Jesus Christ (see John 10:28).

Those are wonderful promises, but you would be rightfully skeptical of them if they were made by a god who had a track record of broken promises. But those promises weren't made by just any god; they were made by the One who is known as the One True God. Those promises were made to you by a God who has a perfect record of kept promises. Why does He keep His promises? Because it is impossible for God to lie (see Hebrews 6:18). He is a God of His Word. He is faithful and true.

God's plan of salvation requires that we put our faith and trust in Jesus Christ. Some people can't get over that hurdle. But their hesitancy must be due to something within them; it can't be because they have found God untrustworthy.

Faithfulness is so much embedded in God's character that it flows over and through those who follow Him. As the Holy Spirit works within the life of every believer, the character of God begins to grow and show. These godly character traits, referred to as "fruits of the Spirit" include faithfulness (see Galatians 5:22–23). When we are faithful, we are reflections of the God who is faithful.

Even though no one has found God untrustworthy, we still may be skeptical about His faithfulness. That's because our own faith may be unreliable from time to time. We say we believe in God, but then we don't act like it; we claim we belong to Him, but our lives don't show it. Consequently, we often mistakenly think that God won't be faithful to us because we haven't been faithful to Him.

But God's promises aren't conditional on *our* performance. Look at the apostle Peter, for example. His performance wasn't stellar. Although he had sufficient faith to get out of the boat, after a few steps on the water he was overcome by fear and his faith sank along with him (see Matthew 14:22–33). After Christ's arrest, Peter was faithless when he denied even knowing his Lord (see Mark 14:66–72). Not a good moment for a disciple of Jesus! Yet God kept all of His promises to Peter and used him to spread the gospel to the world around him after Christ's ascension.

The outcomes of God's promises are not dependent on us holding up some end of the bargain. We didn't have a part of a bargain anyway—except to receive the benefit of God's promises. He makes and keeps His promises based on His character alone.

God is amazing because He makes spectacular promises, and through His inherent faithfulness He relieves us of all anxiety over whether He will keep those promises. So when God makes a promise like, "Come to me, all you who are weary and burdened, and I will give you rest" (Matthew 11:28), He means it.

God doesn't want us to pop a coronary artery from angst over whether He will do what He has promised. He wants us to rest in the assurance of His faithfulness. God's promises made are promises kept.

Chapter 10

God Is All-Powerful

For the Lord God omnipotent reigneth. . .
From George Frideric Handel's *Messiah*

Power is one of those words we've diminished through common usage. Just as we've reduced the word *miracle* to an adjective applied to otherwise common activities or household products (Miracle Whip anyone?), we've turned *power* into something ordinary. There's a power bar, the power lunch, Power Rangers, power words, even the power tie. Big deal!

Actually, it's common for people to think more in terms of strength than of power, and we seem to assign more value to it. There's *StrengthsFinder 2.0*, one of the world's most popular books, and the World's Strongest Man competition, where large Nordic men compete for the title by hoisting tractor tires over their heads.

And don't get us started on the American superhero. Thanks to those ubiquitous comic book characters who have spawned countless movies and even more sequels, we have flawed beings who, when called upon to enact truth, justice, and the American way, are capable of incredible feats of strength.

Maybe that's why the terms *omnipotent* or *all-powerful* as applied to God don't register with us like they should. We're jaded by strength. God is all-powerful? Oh yeah? Can He leap tall buildings in a single bound? Can He save the world from bad guys? Or how about this: can God make a rock so heavy that He couldn't lift it?

How sad that we've trivialized God's omnipotence and now often picture Him as a heavenly hunk rather than who He truly is: *the infinite God possessing infinite power*. Forget about your own infatuation with superhuman strength and with your small conceptions about God's divine power. Here's how amazing He is:

- By the mere power of His spoken word, the universe exploded into existence with a force beyond measure or comprehension.
- By His power the planets stay perfectly aligned, and the sun, 93 million miles from earth, blasts its unimaginable energy in a way that perfectly warms seven billion people.
- Any demonstration of natural power we've witnessed or recorded on this planet—whether hurricane, flood, or volcano—is but a shadow of God's awesome might.

The psalmist David, one of literature's greatest poets, wrote that "power belongs to. . .God" (Psalm 62:11) and "Great is our Lord, and abundant in power" (Psalm 147:5 ESV). But not even this gifted writer could adequately capture God's magnificent power, something that is immeasurable and beyond our imagination. Which is why we need to step outside our mortal selves and stop trying to compare God to our existence or our ability to create fictional characters of extraordinary strength.

God is not an extension of human powers or creative imaginations. When we compare Him to our finite lives, we put limits on Him—or worse, we try to devise stupid thought experiments like the rock thing. God is not limited to or by anything. He is eternal, infinite, and utterly almighty. At the same time, He is personal and longs to share His power with us. His storehouse of power and energy is unlimited, so anything He does for us takes nothing away from Him. His power is not just sufficient for us; it is available in extravagant abundance. Paul the apostle both praises and personalizes the God of power:

Now to him who is able to do immeasurably more than all we ask or imagine, according to his power that is at work within us, to him be glory in the church and in Christ Jesus throughout all generations, for ever and ever!
EPHESIANS 3:20–21

Think about that for a moment. Let the truth of that verse wash over you and astonish you with the thought of this all-powerful God who asks you to think thoughts bigger than you have ever imagined. He is able to—even more, He *wants to*—do even more than that for you. And consider this: God is not limited to what He has already done. He can do even more.

From now on, search for words to describe our amazing God, words that will strengthen your faith and stretch your imagination. When you pray, tell God how thankful you are for His power and might and majesty. And give Him praise for making that power available to you. Pray just as Jesus instructed His followers to pray almost two thousand years ago:

> *"For Yours is the kingdom and the*
> *power and the glory forever. Amen."*
> MATTHEW 6:13 NKJV

CHAPTER 11

GOD IS JEALOUS

"I, the LORD your God, am a jealous God."
EXODUS 20:5

In the previous ten chapters, we have discussed positive, affirmative, and uplifting character traits of God. All of a sudden, it might seem that we're shifting our perspective over to the "dark side" of God's nature with a discussion of His jealousy. After all, jealousy is a disparaged emotion—the "green-eyed monster"—associated with negative thoughts, fears, and anxieties, and it often results in resentment and anger over the anticipated loss of something (or someone) over which (or whom) we assert ownership.

We are not sure how human jealousy starts or how we can stop it, but we know it isn't good. We even know that the Bible doesn't view jealousy as a virtue and warns against it. So how can a perfect God have such a glaring flaw?

There are two sides of jealousy. On one end of the spectrum, it is a beneficial quality; on the other end, it is a detrimental emotion. As sinful people, we're more familiar with the malevolent side of jealousy, so that is what we immediately think of. When *we* are jealous, our emotion is focused on our own self-interest: our wants, our desires, our fears. But the beneficial jealousy—God's jealousy—has as its motivation the interests and protection of others. God isn't jealous for Himself. He is jealous for you. He is only interested in your protection and what is best for you.

When we exhibit a jealousy similar to God's, we don't think of it in terms of our being jealous. Here's an analogy to which you can probably relate.

Suppose you are the parent of an energetic two-year-old daughter. Although she is only a toddler, she can do much more than toddle. She can sprint. At times it seems she can defy gravity and climb walls. To help her expend her energy (so you can preserve your sanity), you take her for a walk around the block. But she is not content to walk. She bolts out the door to explore what for her is uncharted territory. You quickly grab her hand to restrain her propulsion. As you approach the street intersection, her wonder of the unknown does not wane but only increases. She proceeds across the curb with unbridled enthusiasm. You quickly squeeze her hand with a vicelike grasp and nearly yank her shoulder out of its socket as you pull her close to your side and back onto the safety of the sidewalk. You issue a stern proclamation: "No! No running into the street."

Are you being harsh to this young one who remains totally innocent? Absolutely not! You are simply looking out for her well-being.

The next day, the scenario repeats itself. And your daughter still isn't any more savvy to the dangers of crossing the street. So again she starts into the street. Again, you pull her back, but this time you give her tiny hiney a measured swat, just firm enough to get her attention and let her know it isn't an encouraging love-pat. You want to get her attention and instill a Pavlov-like reaction the next time she considers crossing the curb. Are you a horrible parent? Quite the contrary. You are a parent who is exhibiting care, concern, and protection for your daughter.

And so it is with God. His jealousy arises out of an intense and passionate love for you. Accordingly, He wants only what is best for you and devotes Himself to protecting you, often from yourself. Sometimes we absentmindedly and innocently "cross the street," not realizing the danger. Other times, we're running wild in the streets with a rebellious and defiant attitude. Either way, God remains jealous for you.

For us, the "crossing the street" analogy applies to our affections. God is jealous for your love and devotion. It is not an ego issue for Him; it is a matter of knowing and wanting what is best for you. He knows that you are in danger if you are distracted and caught up in a materialistic mind-set. He jealously watches over how you spend your time, the activities in which you engage, and the close relationships you maintain. He knows that you are vulnerable in ways you don't understand. Sometimes He will make His protective plan evident with a "no," and other times His intervention may require divine intervention with a swat on your hiney, figuratively speaking.

Isn't it amazing that the Creator of the Universe is so much in love with you that He is actually jealous for your well-being?

CHAPTER 12

....

GOD IS HOLY

"Holy, holy, holy is the LORD *of hosts,*
the whole earth is full of his glory!"
THE SERAPHIM
ISAIAH 6:3 ESV

At one time or another, we've all wondered what it would be like to be God, to have all His attributes. It's a natural fantasy for us feeble creatures. How else do you explain the success of the film *Bruce Almighty*? By the same token, have you ever considered what it would be like for God to be us? That's not a crazy thought, mainly because God has already done it in the person of Jesus, who was God in human form.

As incredible and amazing as this thought is (we'll talk more about it in Part 3), imagining God walking the earth in the person of Jesus doesn't quite capture what it took for God to become one of us. In his description of the incarnation (the word that describes the act of God becoming human), C. S. Lewis compares the process to something we can easily imagine—probably with disgust. Lewis writes, "If you want to get the hang of it, think how you would like to become a slug or a crab."

Slugs or crabs may not be the most disgusting creatures you could think of, but they come pretty close. Slugs in particular are slimy and creepy and just plain awful. Crabs may not look as repulsive, but they dwell on the bottom of the sea and basically eat garbage. The point of Lewis's comparison is that God becoming us was just plain awful, at least from our perspective. From God's perspective, of course, it's a very different story, because He did not become one of us against His will. Because of His amazing love for us, He *willingly* became a lowly human.

We need to keep something very important in mind: just because God *became* like us doesn't mean He *is* like us. We may share some of His qualities, and He may generously make them available to us, but there is one quality that makes God utterly unlike us: His holiness.

We think of the word *holiness* as that quality of God that makes Him better than us by degrees—as in we are *imperfect* and He is *perfect,* as if we're both on some kind of holiness scale. In truth, God is on an entirely different plane. When it comes to His holiness, He lives in another dimension.

The very definition of the word *holy* gives us a clue. The Hebrew word for the English word *holy* means "to cut or separate." More than any other, this characteristic separates us from God. God isn't just different from us in the way He is; He is also wholly different from us in the way He acts. That's why there is such a great gulf separating us from God. We are sinners, and God is holy. Holiness can never interact with anything unholy.

There's a remarkable passage in the Bible that describes the prophet Isaiah and his terrifying vision of the Most Holy God sitting upon His heavenly throne. You can read it for yourself in Isaiah 6:1–7. What you will find is an astonishing picture of a mortal who is confronted with the holiness of God. "Woe to me!" he says. "I am ruined!" The chasm between him and a holy God fills him with despair. Isaiah recognizes his vast imperfection and cries out, "I am a man of unclean lips, and I live among a people of unclean lips, and my eyes have seen the King, the LORD Almighty."

The implication of these dramatic statements should not be lost on us. Holy isn't just another attribute of God. Holy is what God is. It isn't a standard He must conform to, because He *is* the standard. At the same time, because God is merciful (He doesn't give us what we deserve), His holiness isn't just about Him being different from us. As Michael Horton writes, "It also includes His movement toward us."

Because God is wholly holy, He can't share His holiness with us. He is still "other" than we are. But because God became a human being in the form of Jesus, He identifies with us and calls us to separate ourselves from sin and death and be joined to Him—which we can do when we put our faith in Jesus rather than our own abilities.

The story of Isaiah's vision of the holy God continues as one of the seraphim (winged angelic beings at the scene who call out "Holy, holy, holy") flies to the prophet with a burning coal taken with tongs from the altar. The seraph touches Isaiah's unclean mouth, thereby taking away Isaiah's guilt and atoning for his sin. It is the grace of God dramatically illustrated—God giving Isaiah what he doesn't deserve.

We may not experience Isaiah's excruciating pain when he was confronted with God's holiness, but we should think about it the same way Isaiah did—and worship the Lord for the holy God He is.

PART 2

AMAZING CREATOR

INTRODUCTION

....

God of wonders, beyond our galaxy,
You are holy, holy.
The universe declares your majesty,
You are holy, holy.
STEVE HINDALONG AND MARK BYRD

When you experience something amazing, it's only natural that you want others to enjoy the same experience. You eat at a fantastic new restaurant and you can't wait to tell others. That new mobile phone you stood in line to get? Oh man, it's the best ever, and you just have to share your enthusiasm for your new best friend (your phone) with your old best friend (Sally). And that movie you just saw? It's so popular because people like you tell others about it. It's called "word of mouth"—only these days you're doing it through social media as well as in person.

When you engage in this kind of enthusiastic, unsolicited personal marketing, you become an evangelist for the restaurant, the phone, and the movie. You literally bring "good news" to others. You want them to enjoy and know the benefits and the joy you are experiencing.

It may seem strange to be using the word *evangelist* like this, mainly because the modern stereotype of an evangelist is a person who talks with a loud voice, waves his arms a lot, and often has big hair and a shiny suit. Try not to think of an evangelist or *evangelism* that way. Instead, imagine yourself sharing some very good news with someone else, preferably someone you care about.

Telling a friend or family member about your favorite things and experiences is pretty easy. They have physical properties that someone else can use or experience. But God? You may have (and we hope you do) an incredible story to tell about the amazing God you have personally experienced and all He has done for you.

But how do you share that good news with others in a way that doesn't sound like you believe in fairy tales? How do you tell your friends about the amazing but *invisible* God?

The rules of scientific discovery dictate that testable evidence is necessary for something to be verifiable. The problem—for science, not for God—is that God can't be detected by your senses and therefore can't be tested by any scientific method. But there are other things in life that can't be detected by your senses, and you accept them as real. How about love, for instance? You can't measure love physically, but you can measure its effects. So it is with God. You can't detect His physical properties because there aren't any. But you can see the amazing effects of His being in the world.

In the next dozen chapters, we will explore the wonders and power and majesty of our amazing Creator God. There's much more we could say on each topic, but we hope there's enough here to challenge your mind to learn more and to stir your heart to love God more. And in the process you may just feel compelled to share the good news of what you've learned with someone you care about.

CHAPTER 13

....

SCIENCE AND FAITH

The whole point of Darwinism is to explain the world
in a way that excludes any role for a Creator.
What is being sold in the name of science
is a completely naturalistic understanding of reality.

PHILLIP JOHNSON

Scientists, philosophers, and theologians are pretty much agreed about this: it is the function of science to determine the *facts* of the universe; it is the function of religion to determine its *meaning*. But opinions about the origins of the universe diverge, and arguments become heated, over whether the Bible can be used as a source of scientific information. Secular scientists try to exclude biblical perspectives by limiting the inquiry to what can be tested in a laboratory. It is their position that any belief or theory with any hint of "supernatural" causes must be disregarded. Since God doesn't appear in a telescope or under a microscope, these scientists reject from consideration any theory of a God-caused universe.

But science and faith are not mutually exclusive, and a large (and growing) segment of the scientific community acknowledges this fact. Much is said about the tension between science and faith. The most frequently quoted sources contend that science and faith are incompatible, but many believe that the possible existence of an "intelligent designer" is a legitimate scientific inquiry.

Granted, the Bible is not a science textbook. It was written for the primary purpose of revealing God's plan to establish a relationship with humankind. So it is more focused on who God is and who we are from a relational point of view. While the Bible contains some scientific information, it wasn't intended to explain all scientific intricacies and mathematical formulas. The Bible won't tell you how to clone a sheep; rather, its purpose is to explain how the heavenly Shepherd cares for His flock.

But the Bible is not the only source by which God reveals Himself. The written Word is referred to as the "special revelation of God." But there is also "general revelation" by which God uses the natural world to disclose His existence. By looking at nature in the world around us, we can see evidence of God's handiwork. You don't have to be a geologist or a theoretical physicist to make these discoveries. The wonders of God's creation are readily apparent to all of us if we only look around: "The heavens declare the glory of God; the skies proclaim the work of his hands" (Psalm 19:1).

And the apostle Paul said that God's handprint on the world is so strikingly obvious that people have no excuse for missing it:

For ever since the world was created, people have seen
the earth and sky. Through everything God made,
they can clearly see his invisible qualities—his eternal
power and divine nature. So they have no excuse
for not knowing God.
ROMANS 1:20 NLT

When the Bible does speak about scientific matters, it does so with accuracy. Take, for example, the sequence of creation events (that the universe had a point of beginning, that the atmosphere on earth appeared, followed by plant forms, then fish and birds, after which there came other wildlife and, finally, humans). Astrophysicist Hugh Ross has calculated that the odds of Moses correctly guessing all the details of the origin and proper order of the development of earth (and life on earth) as he specified in chapters 1 and 2 of Genesis are less than one in forty million. The only reasonable explanation is that God divinely inspired the writings of Moses to recount the events that happened eons before Moses was born, but that God Himself initiated.

We have a God who is not dependent upon science

to prove His existence. Neither is He worried that science will contradict it.

CHAPTER 14

....

EVIDENCE FOR GOD

I believe in Christianity as I believe that the Sun has risen,
not only because I see it, but because by it I see everything else.
C.S. LEWIS

The philosopher Bertrand Russell, famous for his adamant disbelief in God, was once asked what he would tell God if he were to die and discover that God really exists. "Not enough evidence, God," Russell replied. "Not enough evidence." That seems to be the issue with many people today, including some very vocal and influential atheists who are not shy about sharing their unbelief. Their biggest beef with God? Like Bertrand Russell, they say there's just not enough evidence to prove He exists.

Rather than react negatively to these new atheists, we'd like to thank them for challenging those of us who say we believe in God to actually *know* He is real. You see, it's one thing to talk about how amazing God is and to feel in our hearts that He exists but quite another to *know* He really exists. Children believe in Santa Claus because they've been told he's jolly and generous. But when they find out he's a fictional character, they lose confidence in Santa as a real person, and he becomes nothing more than a merry myth. The same thing can happen to God if we don't have confidence that He is real.

Don't get us wrong. You can believe in God even if you don't know the evidence for your belief. But at some point, you should be asking yourself if your belief is reasonable. Otherwise you will never have anything more than childlike faith. More crucially, without the confidence that God is a real Person and not just a myth, you won't fully appreciate all the amazing qualities we've written about in this book.

So, thank you Bertrand Russell, Richard Dawkins, Sam Harris, and all you other well-known atheists out there. Thank you for challenging our belief in God. By responding to your unbelief, our belief becomes stronger.

So what about the evidence for God? The good news is that there's plenty. We're going to look at some amazing evidence in the next few chapters, but first we want to give you a word of warning. If you're looking for a "smoking gun" that absolutely proves God's existence, you're not going to find it. But that's okay, because there's no such thing as "complete objectivity" when it comes to belief. The philosopher J.P. Moreland reminds us that the best we can do with 99.9 percent of the beliefs in the world is to say, "It's reasonable to believe." The same is true of your belief in God. If after considering the evidence for God you can say, "A reasonable person would accept that as truth," you are standing on solid ground.

With this in mind, when it comes to evidence for God's existence, think in terms of "clues" instead of "proof." Because He's invisible, God can't be tested in a laboratory, but the clues He has left about His existence can be examined. Think of these clues—whether they are logical, philosophical, scientific, or moral—as strands in a rope. A single strand is not strong enough to bear any significant weight, but when several strands are woven together, the rope becomes much stronger and can bear more weight. So it is with clues and belief. What matters as you look at the evidence for belief is not any one clue but the combined or cumulative strength of several clues woven together.

In the next few chapters we're going to present a number of clues pointing to God's existence. Before you move on, however, we want you to consider a question every person, whether or not he or she believes in God, must consider: *Why is there something rather than nothing?* It may seem like a silly question, but when you're talking about the universe and everything in it, including you, it's a very logical and important one. No matter what you're thinking about right now (a chair, a car, a bird), you can answer the question by saying that the object came from something else. It didn't just appear out of nowhere. Someone made it, or it had a mother.

The name for the logical sequence leading to an object is called *contingency*, which means this: anything that exists is dependent (or contingent) on something else. But this idea of contingency has a problem. The process of contingency has to start with something that isn't contingent, or a first cause. Without that, you would never arrive at the present moment where the chair, the car, and the bird exist.

Mathematicians will tell you that you can't keep going back in a series of infinite causes and events simply because you can't keep going backward to infinity. This is known as "infinite regression," and it's not possible. To get to a *present* thing, you have to have a *first* thing. In the language of philosophy, you have to have a *necessary being*.

How's that for a clue? Read on to discover what this means.

CHAPTER 15

....

GOD WAS HERE FIRST

*If the universe had a beginning, then something external
to the universe must have caused it to come into existence—
something, or Someone, transcendent to the natural world.
As a result, the idea of creation is no longer merely a matter
of religious faith; it is a conclusion based on the most
straightforward reading of the scientific evidence.*
CHARLES COLSON

Science has determined, beyond any doubt, that the
universe had a beginning at a specific point in time. This
is a fairly recent discovery for the scientific community
in particular, and to the rest of the world in general. In
the past, the general idea that the universe had a point
of beginning was not widely accepted, except among
those who believed in the Bible.

Philosophers and most scientists alike have resisted
this theory because it implies that something must

have been the precipitating cause. They subscribed to a theory that the universe existed in a steady-state condition with new matter being formed from that which was already formed. But the relatively recent discovery of the "Big Bang" exploded this "steady-state" theory (pun intended). Now the implications must be addressed.

If there was a beginning of the universe, there must have been a beginner—something or someone had to have caused it. The universe was the effect, so someone had to be the cause. Fred Heeren, a respected science writer, put it this way in his book *Show Me God*: "A series of causes cannot be infinite. There must have been a first cause, which itself is uncaused."

So who or what is the First Big Cause that got the universe started? You can probably answer that question already, but let's pretend you were building a profile for the First Big Cause based on clues that are evident from the nature of the universe.

According to Heeren, the First Big Cause must be:

1. *Independent of the universe itself.* Not only out of the world, but the First Big Cause must be above and beyond all that is in the universe. Things don't make themselves.
2. *All-powerful.* Consider the power output and the quantity of materials that were required to put the universe into place.
3. *Timeless.* Nothing in the universe could predate the universe itself. The First Big Cause must have existed before time as we know it.
4. *Supernatural.* In addition to being beyond our

parameters of time, the First Big Cause must transcend the physical realm of the universe.

5. *Supremely intelligent.* Reflect on the complexities of the components of the universe. Whether it be orbiting planets or your digestive system, these systems work together with great symmetry and harmony. That implies intelligence on the part of the First Big Cause.

6. *Personality.* We don't mean "perky" or "outgoing." Personality refers to a being with intentionality, capable of doing things on purpose.

Does this sound like anyone you know? The Bible proclaims God as the Great Initiator. It says He was the First Big Cause that produced the effect of the universe: "In the beginning God created the heavens and the earth" (Genesis 1:1).

The Bible further describes His characteristics, which show that He perfectly fits the profile scientists have determined would be required of the First Big Cause. See how amazingly His characteristics (listed below in "attribute" terminology) match the profile checklist. According to the Bible, God is:

1. *Transcendent (independent of the universe).* The Old Testament underscores this principle when it says that God existed before the mountains were created (see Psalm 90:2).

2. *Omnipotent (all-powerful).* "You have made the heavens and earth by your great power and outstretched arm. Nothing is too hard for

you" (Jeremiah 32:17).

3. *Eternal (timeless).* God described His own eternal nature when He said, "I am the one who is, who always was, and who is still to come" (Revelation 1:8 NLT).

4. *A Spirit (supernatural).* Because God is a Spirit and does not possess a physical body, He is not limited to our dimensions: "He alone can never die, and he lives in light so brilliant that no human can approach him. No one has ever seen him, nor ever will" (1 Timothy 6:16 NLT).

5. *Omniscient (supreme intelligence).* God knows every scientific truth, even those that humanity has not yet discovered: "How great is our Lord! His power is absolute! His understanding is beyond comprehension!" (Psalm 147:5 NLT).

6. *A Being (personality).* God is not some amorphous "force." He has a will and is capable of feelings: "I AM WHO I AM. . . . This is my name forever, the name you shall call me from generation to generation" (Exodus 3:14–15).

The Bible was written centuries ago, and these character traits of God were recorded long before the scientists of the twentieth and twenty-first centuries developed a profile for the First Big Cause. From about 1500 BC (when Moses wrote Genesis), the Bible has been declaring that God created the universe. Now, about thirty-five hundred years later, the profile of the First Big Cause seems to confirm what the Bible has been saying all along.

CHAPTER 16

....

GOD AND THE BIG BANG

*By faith we understand that the universe was
formed at God's command, so that what is seen
was not made out of what was visible.*

HEBREWS 11:3

We're going to take you on a little journey, all the
way back to the beginning of the universe. Before this
beginning, nothing material existed because the universe didn't exist. When people today—scientists,
philosophers, poets, theologians, or ordinary folks—
think about how it all began, they are at a disadvantage
because they weren't there. Nobody was. Which is why
the all the theories about how the universe got going
are just that—theories.

Scientists try to figure out how the universe
began by the process of discovery and measurement.

Philosophers and poets use logic and art to describe what might have happened. Theologians attempt to explain the beginning by going to Genesis, the Book of Beginnings. In the first verse in this first book of the Bible, in a statement that is both simple and elegant, this explanation for the origin of the universe is offered:

In the beginning God created the heavens and the earth.

If you believe in God, you accept that explanation, even if you don't know how it happened. At the same time, you may be a bit uncomfortable talking about that in mixed company (especially if there are scientists, philosophers, or poets in the room), because you are pretty sure they don't believe that God had anything to do with it. Of course, if they don't believe Genesis 1:1, they need to come up with a better explanation, and it's not like there are a lot of other options. As we see it, there are basically two:

1. *The universe has always existed.* The idea is that the universe didn't have a beginning but has always existed in a "steady state" condition with new matter being formed from that which was already there. There's only one problem with this theory. Because of innovative measuring instruments developed in the last quarter century, such as the Hubble Telescope (1990) and the Cosmic Background Explorer (1992), modern science now accepts the notion that the universe had a beginning. So the first part of Genesis 1:1 is true—or at least compatible with what science believes to be true.

2. *The universe created itself.* The response to this second option for the origin of the universe is more philosophical than scientific. The Latin phrase *ex nihilo, nihil fit*—"from nothing, nothing comes"— refutes the theory as clearly as any experiment. And the fact that no scientific experiment has ever shown something coming from nothing just adds weight to what the philosophers have already said: you can't get something from nothing.

The weakness of these two alternate explanations should turn most thinking people back to the explanation offered in the second part of Genesis 1:1—*God created the heavens and the earth*—but there's still that God thing to contend with, and most in the scientific community aren't willing to go there. Where they are willing to go, however, is to a theory called the Big Bang, a catchy name given to a cataclysmic cosmic event that Steven Weinberg, author of *The First Three Minutes: A Modern View of the Origin of the Universe,* describes as "an explosion which occurred simultaneously everywhere, filling all space from the beginning with every particle of matter rushing apart from every other particle." It was, in the words of Bill Bryson in his popular book *A Short History of Almost Everything,* "instant universe."

Most scientists accept the Big Bang theory, but it begs another question, one that puts us back to square one: *who or what caused the Big Bang?* Bryson acknowledges, "It seems impossible that you could get something from nothing, but the fact that there once was nothing and now there is a universe is evident proof that you can."

Sorry Bill, that's not proof at all, but an avoidance of what's right in front of you.

The most reasonable explanation for the cause of the Big Bang is found once again in Genesis: "And God said, 'Let there be light,' and there was light" (1:3). When God spoke, there was indeed a Big Bang. And it wasn't something God *used* but something He *did*.

The famed astronomer Robert Jastrow acknowledged that the scientific explanation for the beginning of the world lines up with the Genesis account:

The essential elements in the astronomical and biblical account of Genesis is the same; the chain of events leading to man commenced suddenly and sharply, at a definite moment in time, in a flash of light and energy.
ROBERT JASTROW

Can it be proved beyond the shadow of a doubt that God is the originator of the Big Bang and therefore the Creator of the universe? No, but as we've said, very few "truths" in our world can be proven that way. The reality is that some faith is required for everything you believe in, whether it's the Big Bang theory or something as ordinary as starting your car. So it isn't so much about putting your faith in theories as it is about believing in the object of those theories.

If science or your car or any other man-made object is worthy of belief, then that's where you should go. But if the amazing God we've written about is worthy of your belief, then we invite you to do just that. Science is a wonderful tool meant to discover and explain the origin of our world. But only God is the one true Originator.

CHAPTER 17

A PRETTY FINE UNIVERSE

The human mind is not capable of grasping the Universe. We are like a little child entering a huge library. The walls are covered to the ceilings with books in many different tongues. The child knows that someone must have written these books. It does not know who or how. It does not understand the languages in which they are written. But the child notes a definite plan in the arrangement of the books—a mysterious order which it does not comprehend, but only dimly suspects.
ALBERT EINSTEIN

Yes, God loves you and has proved that fact by allowing His Son to die that you might have eternal life. But God's love is also demonstrated in many ways we tend to take for granted. How about the environments in which you live? We'll start by looking at the grand universe (and in the next chapter, we'll narrow our focus to just our solar system and Planet Earth).

Scientists have determined that there are twenty-five or so parameters that must be fixed ("constant") if life is to exist. If any one of these is missing, then life is impossible. Here is only a partial list:

- *The gravitational force in the universe must remain constant at its present level.* If it were stronger than it is, then the stars would be too hot, and they would burn up quickly and unevenly. If it were weaker than it is, then stars would remain so cool that nuclear fusion—the process by which stars, including our own sun, create energy—would never happen. And you wouldn't want to be stuck with that problem.
- *The expansion rate of the universe must remain constant.* The universe has been expanding ever since the Big Bang. If the expansion rate occurred at a faster rate, no galaxies would have been able to form. If the rate were slower, then the universe would have collapsed prior to formation—or your formation, for that matter.
- *The velocity of light must be constant.* If light traveled faster, the stars would be too luminous for us to tolerate. If light traveled slower, the stars (including the sun) would not be luminous enough.

The list continues, covering everything from the ratio between protons and electrons, to the proximity and frequency of supernova eruptions (a supernova is a cataclysmic explosion of a massive star in which most of the star is blown off into interstellar space). If the eruptions were too close or too frequent or occurred too soon, then the radiation would exterminate life on the planet. If the eruptions were too far away or too infrequent or too late, then there would not be enough heavy element ashes for the formation of rocky planets.

Dr. Hugh Ross uses the term "fine-tuning" when he describes the conditions that must be present in the universe to permit life. That reference is both accurate and descriptive. A little bit of difference in any direction would be catastrophic. As it is, God made everything "just right."

The "just right" parameters for life in the universe are very narrow. For example, if the strong nuclear force were just 0.3 percent stronger or 0.2 percent weaker, the universe would never be able to support life. The expansion rate of the universe has an even tighter parameter. Life wouldn't be possible in a universe that had an expansion rate different than ours by more than one part out of 10 to the 55th power. You know that one millionth of a percent (0.000001) is infinitesimal. So, imagine another 50 or so zeros tucked into that percentage. That is fine-tuning at its most delicate.

Why does all of this matter? If you believe that the universe is merely the result of random, unplanned chance, then it is no big deal. It is the way that it is. But if you believe that God created and fine-tuned the universe intentionally with you (and the rest of humanity) in mind, then God's creativity, power, and complexity—not to mention His personal interest in the human race—should amaze you.

CHAPTER 18

....

OUR AMAZING SOLAR SYSTEM AND JUST-RIGHT EARTH

The heavens declare the glory of God; the skies proclaim the work of his hands. Day after day they pour forth speech; night after night they reveal knowledge.

PSALM 19:1–2

The universe isn't the only aspect of the cosmos that has to be finely tuned to permit life. Let's bring our analysis a little closer to home. By "closer," we mean our own solar system.

Most of us live fairly comfortably in our solar system, but that wouldn't be the case in any other known solar system. All solar systems are not created equal when it comes to supporting life. Our sun is not just a plain ol' star among the billions of others in the Milky Way Galaxy. Our sun has a planetary system (the "solar system"), which is made up of the earth and seven other planets—along with the various planetary moons, asteroid belts, and the recently demoted Pluto. Our solar system has certain features that allow life, but these features are not common to all other solar systems. Here are the unique features of our solar system for which you can thank God:

- *A solar system that has one, and only one, star.* With more than one star, tidal interactions would throw the Planet Earth's orbit out of whack. If we had no star, then the planet would be a frozen mass that could not support life.
- *A solar system with a star of the right age.* Newly formed stars have burning rates and temperatures that fluctuate. But if your star is too old, then the luminosity rate changes too quickly to allow life.
- *A star in your solar system that is the correct size.* If a solar system's star is too large, then you have those pesky luminosity fluctuations that keep its planets from supporting life. Too small, and you've got a host of other problems, such as tidal forces that knock the planet's rotational period out of sync and not enough ultraviolet radiation for plants. Ninety-nine percent of all stars are the wrong size for what you're looking for in a life-supporting solar system.
- *A star that is the correct distance from the planet.* If a planet is too far away from its star, then the temperature on the planet's surface

would be too cool to permit a stable water evaporation cycle. Too close, and the climate is too warm to allow a stable water evaporation cycle. If the distance between the earth to the sun differed by just 2 percent, then no life would be possible. This parameter eliminates 99 percent of all stars as candidates for a solar system that humans could call home.

Now, let's get really up close and personal and see the permissible parameters for life on our own planet. All of the following factors affect the viability of life on this planet. A change in the parameters of any one of them would either prevent the existence of life—or make it extremely unpleasant:

- *The orbital pattern around the sun*: a change could produce extreme variations that would make life impossible.
- *The tilt of the earth's axis*: the differential in the surface temperature would be too extreme.
- *The speed of the earth's rotation*: temperature changes and wind velocities would be too great.
- *The age of the earth*: if the earth were much younger, then it would rotate too fast. If it were much older, it would rotate too slowly.
- *The ratio of oxygen to nitrogen in the earth's atmosphere*: life functions would be severely impacted by any change in this ratio.

Is it pure dumb luck that we humans landed on Planet Earth, or could life be the same (or better) if we had landed somewhere else? Don't pack your bags yet, because you may not have many options. Unlike our own solar system, most stars have only one planet in their respective systems. It has been estimated that there might be a trillion galaxies, with possibly one hundred billion stars per galaxy. With one planet per star, that gives us the prospect of one hundred billion trillion planets. According to Dr. Hugh Ross, the odds of getting all the necessary factors for the existence of life on a single planet are one trillionth of a trillionth of a trillionth of a trillionth of 1 percent. But you've only got one hundred billion trillion available planets. The odds *against* finding another suitable planet are astronomical.

This ought to tell you two things: First, you don't have any realistic options for living on any other planet. Second, you should revel in the knowledge that God was so precise and intentional in placing you on a planet that was tailor-made for human existence.

CHAPTER 19

....

IRREDUCIBLE COMPLEXITY

If it could be demonstrated that any complex organ existed which could not possibly have been formed by numerous, successive, slight modifications, my theory would absolutely break down
CHARLES DARWIN

One of the best ways to observe the immensity and power of our amazing God is by looking at the nighttime sky. The psalmist David, standing on his balcony at night, gazed at the dazzling array of stars above him and then wrote:

The heavens declare the glory of God;
the skies proclaim the work of his hands.
Day after day they pour forth speech;
night after night they reveal knowledge.
They have no speech, they use no words;

> *no sound is heard from them.*
> *Yet their voice goes out into all the earth;*
> *their words to the ends of the world.*
> PSALM 19:1–4

David would have been able to see about three thousand stars—the same number you can see today with the naked eye on a clear night free of light pollution. That's a lot of stars, but it's an infinitesimal fraction of the number that actually exist—somewhere between one hundred and four hundred billion in our galaxy alone. When you consider that there are *as many as a trillion* galaxies out there, the number of stars is beyond comprehension.

The world above is truly amazing, but the world within is nothing to sneeze at. We're talking about the world under your nose, in your own body. There's no way David would have known about the incredible complexity that exists in this inner world. We can know, yet we don't give it so much as a second thought. We want to change that. Even if we just scratch the surface, we want to help you think about what's under your skin. In particular, we want to focus on cells, those tiny organisms that do the work of making living things live.

Molecular biologists tell us there are approximately forty trillion cells in the average human body. These cells are like little machines producing the stuff of life. Michael Behe is a respected biochemist who has done pioneering work on the nature of cells. He introduced the concept known as "irreducible complexity," a fancy way of saying that all living things, including you, are composed of molecular "biological machines" that work together to produce a system of interacting parts that in turn produce a basic function.

The human eye is an example of a basic function. It works because millions and millions of cells work together to produce sight. And here's the thing about these molecular biological machines: all the functions have to be there to produce the intended result. If any one of the parts is missing, the system—in this case your eye—does not work. In effect, the human eye is an irreducibly complex biological system, and it's just one example of the vast number of such systems in your body.

Because the parts or systems of a cell can't get any simpler, scientists have a big problem when they try to explain how these systems got here. The most common explanation, one taught in every science textbook, is that the systems evolved. But that's not a satisfactory explanation. Continuing to use the eye as an example, if the system that produces sight evolved over millions of years, at what point did it actually work? Were all creatures with eyes blind until a specific time when the right parts were suddenly in place, and then—*viola!*—there was sight? Seems like a stretch. Behe explains: "Now the thing about irreducibly complex systems is that they cannot be produced by numerous small steps, because one does not acquire the function until close to the end, or at the end. Therefore, with irreducibly complex systems, they cannot be produced by Darwinian evolution."

Anyone looking at the facts needs to at least be open to the alternate explanation, one that happens to also be the most plausible. The reason these irreducibly complex systems work, and the reason they functioned for the first time *at the same time* is because our amazing God made it so. He is the one who "knit together" the wonderfully complex systems in your body that enable you to see and do everything else that makes you human. Most importantly, He gave you a mind to know Him and a heart to love Him.

Chapter 20

....

Amazing DNA

As the director of the Human Genome Project, I have led a consortium of scientists to read out the 3.1 billion letters of the human genome, our own DNA instruction book. As a believer, I see DNA, the information molecule of all living things, as God's language, and the elegance and complexity of our own bodies and the rest of nature as a reflection of God's plan.
Francis S. Collins, M.D., Ph.D

At the end of the twentieth century, the leading spokesperson for atheism was British philosopher Dr. Antony Flew. By 2004, he had changed his position and stated: "Super-intelligence is the only good explanation for the origin of life and the complexity of nature." What triggered this drastic shift in perspective? In large part, he was persuaded by discoveries arising from DNA research.

Beginning in 1953, scientists discovered the

genetic structure deep inside the nucleus of our cells. This genetic material is referred to as DNA, an abbreviation for deoxyribonucleic acid. The discovery of the double-helix structure of the DNA molecule was only the beginning. Embedded within the molecule is an actual code.

DNA coding is similar to computer program coding. Computer programming uses a series of ones and zeros. These two digits repeat in an arranged series called a binary code. The sequencing and ordering constitutes the specific code. The DNA molecule contains four chemicals, which are abbreviated with the letters A, T, G, and C. The sequence and order of these four chemicals create the code using the four letters like the ones and zeros in binary coding. The sequences of these chemicals provide the instructions necessary to assemble complex protein molecules that, in turn, help form structures as diverse as eyes, kidneys, and feet.

Now, prepare yourself to be amazed as you comprehend the magnitude of this:

- Within the tiny space where the DNA molecule resides in every cell of your body, the DNA code is 3.1 billion letters long. (That's a lot of repeating A, T, G and Cs.) If you were to read the code for the DNA information in a single cell—reading at the rate of three letters per second—it would take thirty-one years, assuming you read continually every day, for twenty-four hours a day.
- The amount of information in human DNA

is roughly equivalent to twelve sets of *The Encyclopaedia Britannica*—which would be an incredible 384 volumes' worth of detailed information that would fill forty-eight feet of library shelves.

- The actual thickness of the DNA molecule is only two millionths of a millimeter. According to biologist Michael Denton, a teaspoon of DNA could contain all the information needed to build the proteins for all the species of organisms that have ever lived on the earth, and "there would still be enough room left for all the information in every book ever written."

- Each person's DNA code is unique. Yet 99.9 percent of our DNA is similar to the genetic makeup of everyone else. That means that 0.1 percent difference in the sequencing in those 3.1 billion letters embedded in your cells is what makes you uniquely you.

From a spiritual perspective, the significance of this DNA research is twofold. First, in the debate over origins, it weighs very heavily in favor of an intelligent Designer. God is revealing Himself to the world, and it is becoming obvious to everyone.

At a ceremony acknowledging the accomplishments of the Human Genome Project, President Bill Clinton said, "Today we are learning the language in which God created life. We are gaining ever more awe for the complexity, the beauty, the wonder of God's most divine and sacred gift." Dr. Francis Collins, the Director of the Human Genome Project, responded: "It is humbling for me and awe inspiring to realize that we have caught the first glimpse of our own instruction book, previously known only to God."

But second, and perhaps more importantly, DNA research reaches every individual at a personal level. It reveals God's involvement in our individual lives. Our amazing God wrote a unique, personal genetic code for each of us. While the psalmist David didn't know anything about DNA or genetic coding, he understood the truth they demonstrate as he wrote:

For you created my inmost being; you knit me together in my mother's womb. I praise you because I am fearfully and wonderfully made; your works are wonderful, I know that full well. My frame was not hidden from you when I was made in the secret place.
PSALM 139:13–15

CHAPTER 21

···

MADE IN GOD'S IMAGE

What are mere mortals that you should think about them,
human beings that you should care for them?
Yet you made them only a little lower than God
and crowned them with glory and honor.
PSALM 8:4–5 NLT

If ever the human race needed the kind of humility
King David expressed in Psalm 8, it's now. Rather
than appreciating our amazing God for who He is—
the remarkable all-everything, holy God who created a
beautiful universe for us to live in, who loves us despite
our stubborn and sinful natures—many people use
Him like a genie for stuff they want or as an emergency
kit when things go bad. And when things don't go
their way or something horrible happens in the world
that they can't explain, they make God the scapegoat.

Rather than treating God with respect, they regard Him as an object of scorn. The problem is that most people think too much of themselves and too little of God.

The way to reverse this thinking is to adopt David's perspective. Every once in a while, we need to ask God some questions: "Why do You think about us? Why do You put up with us when we are so insignificant compared to You? Why do You love us when we are so arrogant and rebellious?"

The answer to the last question naturally informs the answers to the others. God loves us because it's His nature to love, and out of that love He created us unlike anything else He made. When you read the first chapter of Genesis and the description of how God made humankind, it is clear we were special from the start: "So God created mankind in his own image, in the image of God he created them; male and female he created them" (Genesis 1:27).

When you consider the implications of this amazing verse, it's not difficult to understand why God thinks about us. We aren't at all insignificant to Him. The very fact that God handcrafted us rather than "calling" us into existence (the way He created the universe) shows that our Maker personally and lovingly formed us. Even more, God made us *in His image*. This doesn't mean we are God or even like God. We are more like hand-signed photographs reflecting His image and bearing His imprint. Consequently, we have several unique qualities that no other living creatures possess. We alone:

- Can communicate with God
- Have the right and responsibility to manage the earth's resources and to rule over all living things (see Genesis 1:26, 28–30)
- Are morally responsible to obey God
- Have both a physical and spiritual dimension

Because of these unique qualities our amazing God has given us, we alone can have a relationship with Him. He calls us by name and cares for us unconditionally. He connects with us with a depth of love and familiarity we experience only in our closest human relationships. But even our earthly interactions are but a shadow of what it is like to feel God's presence in our lives.

Imagine what it was like for our first human ancestors, Adam and Eve, to walk and talk with God like close friends (see Genesis 3:8). That intimacy was broken because God's human creation, gifted with free will, thought it wasn't enough to reflect God's image. They wanted to be just like God. For that transgression they paid a dear price—we all did—as the fellowship with the divine was broken.

But in His great love and mercy, God reached out, giving of Himself with such sacrifice that it is difficult to comprehend. Incredibly, He made it possible for His beloved human children to again walk and talk with Him, though yet imperfectly while sin is still present in the world, but with the promise that someday we will be with Him perfectly and completely:

*And I heard a loud voice from the throne saying,
"Look! God's dwelling place is now among the people,
and he will dwell with them. They will be his people,
and God himself will be with them and be their God.
He will wipe away every tear from their eyes.
There will be no more death or mourning or crying
or pain, for the old order of things has passed away."*
REVELATION 21:3–4

CHAPTER 22

....

THE HUMAN MIND

*One of the stinging criticisms made against Christians
is that their minds are narrow and their hearts are small.*
A.W. TOZER

God didn't expend all of His creativity and power in the formation of the universe. He has an endless supply of each, so there was plenty still available when He created the human brain. Like the universe, the brain is intricate, complex, and amazing beyond our understanding. Upon first examining a human brain (let's not speculate about the circumstances that give you this opportunity), you might consider it a rather unpromising body organ. It would look like a three-pound lump of tofu, consisting of 75 percent water. But don't let its outward appearance fool you:

- The human brain consists of approximately

one hundred billion neurons—about the same number as the stars in the Milky Way Galaxy. Information flows from one neuron to another neuron across a synapse. Each neuron has between a thousand and ten thousand synapses, meaning the brain contains about one quadrillion synapses. If all of the neurons in a human brain were lined up, they would stretch six hundred miles.

- While a person is awake, the human brain generates enough energy to power a low-voltage light bulb.

- An axon is a long and slender nerve fiber that conducts electrical impulses away from the neuron; its function is to transmit information to different neurons. A twenty-year-old man has approximately 109,000 miles of axons in his brain, enough to wrap around the earth's equator four-and-a-half times.

- There are more than one hundred thousand chemical reactions happening in the human brain every second.

- The brain contains approximately one hundred thousand miles of blood vessels. It uses 20 percent of the body's total blood.

- Scientists consider the human brain the most complicated and mysterious thing in the universe. They know and understand more about stars exploding billions of light years away than they know about the human brain.

We can be awed by the intricate complexity of God's design of the brain. But that begs the question: What was God's purpose in doing so? While the Bible doesn't give any anatomical or scientific descriptions of the brain's function, there is much in Scripture about how God intends for us to use our minds.

God wants us to use our minds as tools in moving from our old nature into a Christlike mind-set: "Do not conform to the pattern of this world, but be transformed by the renewing of your mind" (Romans 12:2).

How does this renewal process occur? Remember that old computer programming axiom, Garbage In, Garbage Out? We should be careful about what goes into our minds because it determines the direction of our lives. That is why the apostle Paul wrote:

- "Whatever is true, whatever is noble, whatever is right, whatever is pure, whatever is lovely, whatever is admirable— if anything is excellent or praiseworthy— think about such things" (Philippians 4:8).
- "Set your minds on things above, not on earthly things" (Colossians 3:2).

God has arranged to reveal Himself to us through a wireless connection with our minds so that we can understand His nature. This is truly incredible. Through the Holy Spirit, we can have the mind of Christ:

These are the things God has revealed to us by his Spirit.
The Spirit searches all things, even the deep things of
God. For who knows a person's thoughts except their own
spirit within them? In the same way no one knows the
thoughts of God except the Spirit of God. What we have
received is not the spirit of the world, but the Spirit who
is from God, so that we may understand what God has
freely given us. This is what we speak, not in words taught
us by human wisdom but in words taught by the Spirit,
explaining spiritual realities with Spirit-taught words.
The person without the Spirit does not accept the things
that come from the Spirit of God but considers them
foolishness, and cannot understand them because they are
discerned only through the Spirit. The person with the
Spirit makes judgments about all things, but such a person
is not subject to merely human judgments, for,
"Who has known the mind of the Lord
so as to instruct him?"
But we have the mind of Christ.
1 CORINTHIANS 2:10–16

CHAPTER 23

....

DESIGNED FOR DISCOVERY

For since the creation of the world God's invisible
qualities—his eternal power and divine nature—
have been clearly seen, being understood from what has
been made, so that people are without excuse.

THE APOSTLE PAUL

ROMANS 1:20

One of the ironies of our world is that the people who
are least likely to believe in God are often those most
eager to believe in extraterrestrial life. Carl Sagan,
who championed a Godless universe in his landmark
television series *Cosmos,* was one of the prime movers
behind the government's SETI program—the Search
for Extraterrestrial Intelligence—to find evidence
for life "out there" beyond our own "ordinary" solar
system.

Because of the vast size and great age of the universe,

it is assumed that there's life out there. We just haven't found it yet. The great irony, however, is that there *is* life "out there," but it's not E.T. And even though we can't see Him, there is compelling evidence that this extraterrestrial Being has made it possible for us to live on a just-right planet in a just-right solar system in a just-right universe that isn't ordinary at all. In fact, it's quite extraordinary.

Could there be other worlds like ours, worlds teeming with life? Anything is possible. A God big enough and powerful enough and smart enough to create our planet could create other worlds suitable for life. But all we have is this one, so that's what we should focus on. When we do, we observe a unique universe and a unique home planet with qualities that make it possible for us to live and thrive. Not only that, it's a planet that makes it possible for us to discover how everything works and how everything got here.

Remember those parameters for life we talked about in the chapters on our fine-tuned universe, amazing solar system, and just-right Planet Earth? Not only are those parameters necessary for *habitability*, they are also necessary for *measurability*. Another way of saying it is this: God wants His universe to be discovered because He wants us to discover Him through what He has made. David understood this and wrote, "The heavens declare the glory of God; the skies proclaim the work of his hands. Day after day they pour forth speech; night after night they reveal knowledge" (Psalm 19:1–2).

The more we discover about our fine-tuned habitat, the more amazing it gets. It's possible it all came about by chance and chaos, but a more reasonable explanation is that it was caused by a super-intelligent being with power and wisdom beyond our imagination. But don't just take our word for it. Do some research. Read the data for yourself, watch videos, attend lectures, and talk to scientists. You live in an astounding age, when new information is readily available because of the technology now being employed to discover and measure our universe. Because of the supercomputer you carry around with you (you call it your phone, but in reality it's a supercomputer), you literally have the world in your hands.

It's great to have this capability, but unless you take another step and discover the amazing Creator behind the creation, you will fail to put everything you know in its proper context. The universe didn't get here by chance, and neither did you. The world around you was designed for discovery, and you were designed to discover. As Lee Strobel states in his excellent book *A Case for a Creator,* "don't let the greatest discovery of your life pass you by."

And don't get so focused on these amazing clues for God's existence and the marvelous world He has made that you miss the reason He made it. He wants to have a relationship with you, and that's something you can't accept unless you exercise faith.

Faith does not replace your belief but completes it. Faith is not a substitute for reason but a complement to it. In its simplest form, faith is about trust, and faith in God is a decision to trust Him. You can have all the evidence in the world and still refuse to put your trust in God because you aren't willing to turn your life over to Him. When you come to God in faith, you are saying "Not my will, but Yours." You are telling God, "My works aren't good enough. I need You to make my life work."

When you get to that point, something amazing—even miraculous—happens. It's difficult to explain and impossible to prove apart from your own testimony, but it's as real as anything you will ever know and experience.

CHAPTER 24

....

GOD'S AMAZING MIRACLES

*"Today for show and tell, I've brought a tiny miracle of nature:
a single snowflake! I think we might all learn a lesson from how
this utterly unique and exquisite crystal turns into an ordinary,
boring molecule of water just like every other one when you bring
it into the classroom. And now, while the analogy sinks in,
I will be leaving you drips and going outside. . ."*
CALVIN, FROM THE CARTOON
"CALVIN AND HOBBES" BY BILL WATTERSON

By their very nature, miracles are amazing. By Wikipedia's definition, a "miracle" is "an event not ascribable to human power or the laws of nature and consequently attributed to a supernatural, especially divine, agency." Miracles are amazing because they are acts and events outside the realm of our natural experience that we are incapable of accomplishing by ourselves.

You've been reading about God's miracles for the last eleven chapters. We'll all agree that we've covered some amazing supernatural phenomena—everything from the macro (the Big Bang) to the microscopic (DNA). God's hand in these matters is undeniable. His sense of creativity, beauty, symmetry, and design—down to the most intricate, infinitesimal detail—is astonishing. So how can it be that our lives often seem humdrum and mundane? How can we meander about in a world teeming with God's wonder in all directions and be oblivious to it all?

Although it is not an excuse or an acceptable explanation, this malady of being unmindful of God's miracles is not unique to our generation. Even the disciples, who walked side-by-side with Jesus, were quick to forget the miraculous that took place in their presence.

In chapter 14 of the Gospel of Matthew, the historical account of Christ's feeding of the five thousand is presented. Actually, there were many more than five thousand people there; that is just the number of *men* who were present. This crowd of men, women, and children on the hillsides near Galilee probably totaled closer to eight thousand. And from this collective group, the disciples could scrounge up just five small dinner rolls and two fish fillets. But this paltry foodstuff was no impediment for Jesus. He miraculously multiplied the provisions into a bounty that satiated the entire crowd. There was food in abundance, with enough leftovers to fill twelve baskets.

The disciples were the ones who distributed the miracle-made food to the crowds. They kept returning to Jesus as He produced more and more. Imagine their astonishment with each delivery trip among the throng. So you might think they would never forget this amazing miracle. But you'd be wrong.

In the next chapter, Matthew 15, we read of the account of a similar miracle. This time, there are four thousand men present, plus women and children. The people had been following Jesus for several days, and everyone was hungry and without food. Jesus wanted to feed the crowd because they would faint along the way if they had to walk home without nourishment.

When Jesus called the disciples to take action, they were perplexed with the futility of the situation and answered, "Where could we get enough bread in this remote place to feed such a crowd?" (Matthew 15:33). As it turns out, the crowd coughed up seven small loaves of bread and a few small fish. This was enough for Christ to use in a repeat of His miracle-feeding capabilities. As before, all of the people were fed and went home with full stomachs.

The Bible doesn't record what Jesus said to His disciples afterward, but it's not hard to imagine Him shaking His head and thinking, *Those disciples. . .they can't even remember what I did two pages ago. They are so quick to forget the miracles I have done.*

There is a lesson for us in the forgetfulness of the disciples. We are the same way. When our attention is directed toward God's miracles, we gladly affirm

His mighty powers. But left on our own, we cavalierly ignore those same wonders. The solution is to live in the constant recollection of all that God has done:

I will remember the deeds of the LORD; yes,
I will remember your miracles of long ago.
I will consider all your works and meditate on all
your mighty deeds. . . . You are the God who performs
miracles; you display your power among the peoples.
PSALM 77:11–12, 14

Though He is deserving of it, God doesn't need our affirmation. But we should live in a mental state of awareness of His amazing miraculous power—so that we may have a heart of gratitude and be comforted by the knowledge of His power and care.

PART 3

AMAZING JESUS

INTRODUCTION

··

*The idea of a spiritual heart transplant is a vivid image to me;
once you have the heart of somebody else inside you, then that
heart is there. Jesus' heart is inside me, and my heart is gone.
So if God were to place a stethoscope against my chest,
he would hear the heart of Jesus Christ beating.*

Max Lucado

Imagine that we are living in the year 1 BC and
that we are seeking earnestly to connect with God.
Any mental picture we might hold of the invisible,
intangible God would be a clumsy sketch of the real
thing. Any intellectual understanding we might arrive
at of God's true nature would never be more than
just a beginning, just an inkling. In other words, our
concept of God could be foundational, but it would
be sorely deficient.

So what did God do as a remedy?

Amazingly, He took on a human body and a name:
Jesus, son of Mary and Joseph. As unbelievable as it

sounds, the almighty God, the Creator of the universe, humbled Himself and lived through diapers, bullies, pimples, and the traumas of adolescence.

As a young man, He sweat under the hot sun and got dusty walking along country roads. He enjoyed the friendship of His compatriots; they laughed together, but they also endured threats and condemnation.

Jesus was embraced by the powerless of society—the poor, the crippled, and the outcasts—but He was demonized and viciously attacked by the religious leaders, who strategized to kill Him in order to protect their prestigious positions.

Whether they were for Him or against Him, the people with whom He came in contact were amazed, astonished, and astounded at the things Jesus said and did:

- *He claimed to be God in human form, and He performed what appeared to be supernatural phenomena to prove it.* If He was a fraud, then how else could those apparent miracles be explained?
- *He predicted that He would rise from the dead.* After His crucifixion and burial, hundreds of people saw Him in public.
- *He accepted worship as if He was God, yet He also established friendships with the criminal element of society.* He extended an invitation for all people, regardless of their personal history or social standing, to engage in and

close, intimate relationship with Him. He invited them to come "as you are" without any pre-imposed conditions.

These three distinctives about Jesus Christ set Christianity apart from all other religions. He enunciated the basis for what is known as "the Gospel of Jesus Christ"—that Jesus came to rescue us because we were wandering like lost sheep. He even described Himself as "the good shepherd" who lays down His life for His sheep (John 10:14–15). Our human sin had separated us from the Holy God. We were lost. But Jesus, the God-Man, came to earth to pay the price for sin and bring us back into God's fold.

In the following twelve chapters, we'll examine the life of Jesus to find what it was about Him that so frequently caused responses like this one:

The crowd was amazed and asked, "Could it be that Jesus is the Son of David, the Messiah?"
MATTHEW 12:23 NLT

CHAPTER 25

....

GOD IN THE FLESH

The Word became flesh and made his dwelling among us.
JOHN 1:14

For all the amazing aspects of God's being, character, and personality—His infinite power, knowledge, wisdom, love, grace, and mercy—the most amazing of all just might be the Incarnation. It is staggering to think about a perfect God taking on imperfect human form, the infinite becoming finite, the immortal taking on mortality, the invisible God becoming visible through His Son, Jesus Christ.

God coming to earth in the form of a lowly human being is such a profound mystery, and so unexpected, that even today, two thousand years after it happened, people still struggle to understand how it was possible. Even followers of Christ often fail to grasp the significance of the Incarnation. Once a year they, along with the rest of the world, are reminded of this event when they celebrate Christmas, but the true implications of what the birth of Jesus means are generally lost amidst the pageantry, decorations, and gift giving.

John Newton, a former slave trader, understood what it all meant when he composed the world's most popular hymn:

> *Amazing grace, how sweet the sound,*
> *That saved a wretch like me.*
> *I once was lost, but now I'm found,*
> *Was blind, but now I see!*

Every once in a while, singers of the hymn will substitute "someone" for "wretch," so as not to offend people. But that's missing the point. Newton wrote the song when he was confronted with his own wretchedness in light of God's holiness. He understood that a great unbridgeable gulf exists between a holy God and sinful man, and that the only thing that could ever cross that gulf, giving us humans our only chance of being "saved," is God's amazing grace.

As summarized in the world's most popular Bible verse, that grace was expressed most dramatically and effectively when God gave us His only Son: "For God so loved the world that he gave his one and only Son, that whoever believes in him shall not perish but have eternal life" (John 3:16).

The incredible benefits of the Incarnation can be seen in what God accomplished by becoming human. As A.W. Tozer says so well, God came to dwell *with* us in person so He could be united *to* us, only to ultimately dwell *in* us, so that even now, two millennia after Jesus left the earth, He is still present in each person who calls Him Lord and Savior.

While He was on earth, Jesus lived out the mystery of the Incarnation by being both man and God. At no time in His thirty-plus years of earthly existence was Jesus never fully human *and* fully divine. He had a human body, a human mind, and human emotions.

The people who knew Him as He was growing up—including His own family—didn't believe in Him. They certainly didn't think He was God (see John 7:5). To them, He was just a carpenter's son. Yet when Jesus began His public ministry, He defied the natural world by performing supernatural acts. He turned water into wine, fed thousands of people with a sack lunch, healed the sick, and raised the dead. Once, when Jesus calmed a raging storm just by speaking, His astonished followers were terrified because they realized they were in the presence of God (see Mark 4:41).

People today will often acknowledge that Jesus was a great teacher, a good man, and a fine example for us to follow. But to leave Him as just that is to tragically miss the whole point. That baby born in a manger was a frail human who grew in human wisdom and stature, but He was also almighty God, the Creator of the universe, the Lamb of God without blemish who came to seek and to save the lost. To leave Him in that manger and disregard the amazing implications of what His coming to earth means for all people for all time is to miss the very reason God became flesh. He did it for us.

Tozer concludes:

God loves us and cares for us. God has a plan for us and is in fact carrying out that way. Jesus has set forth God before us. He revealed God's grace, mercy, good and redemptive intention. He set forth, brought it and gave it to us. Now we have only to turn and believe and accept and take and follow. And it is ours.

CHAPTER 26

....

THE MESSIAH NOBODY WANTED

*[W]hile not every text in the Old Testament is about Christ,
the dominating theme of the Old Testament is about Christ
and the fact that He is the coming Messiah. That is central to any
understanding of the Old Testament that is at all accurate.
The promised one of the Old Testament is referred to as the Messiah.*
JOHN MACARTHUR

All through the Old Testament, God promised the Jews that He would send a Rescuer who would establish God's kingdom on earth. This coming deliverer was referred to as "the Messiah." He would be God coming down to earth. Those writings sometimes characterized the Messiah as a prophet who would be speaking for God; other times the references of the future Messiah seem to characterize Him as a priest; still other references cast Him as a king.

But as the time between the pronouncements of the

Messiah and His actual arrival dragged on and on—for hundreds of years—the Jews became more and more certain that this promised Messiah was going to be the Rescuer and Deliverer. They anticipated that He would free them from the oppression under which they lived at the hands of pagan and hostile governments. By the first century AD, the oppressor was the Roman government.

Predictions in the Old Testament as to the personal identity of the Messiah were many and particular. The prophecies the Old Testament prophets proclaimed gave clues as to how the Messiah could be identified: where and when He would be born, His family tree, when and how He would die, and more. Some of these clues were rather generic, with criteria that many people could satisfy; other clues were so specific that few people could meet the test; still other predictions required supernatural intervention that would immediately rule out any imposter:

- The Messiah would be a direct descendant of the famous King David.
- The Messiah had to be born in the hayseed town of Bethlehem.
- The Messiah would be born of a virgin.
- The Messiah would say certain words as He was dying.
- The Messiah would come back from the dead.

There are approximately three hundred references to the Messiah in the Old Testament writings, and within those verses there are approximately forty clues about the Messiah's identity. In 1963 Peter Stoner, a mathematics professor at Westmont College, did extensive research on the probabilities (odds) of the Old Testament's Messiah prophecies applying to Jesus. His research was presented to a Committee of the American Scientific Affiliation, which verified that his calculations were dependable and accurate. Professor Stoner calculated that the odds of one man—Jesus, or anyone else—satisfying only eight of these prophecies were one in 100,000,000,000,000,000. (If you are counting, that's seventeen zeros, which is one hundred thousand trillion.)

Given the fact that the Jews had been waiting hundreds of years for the Messiah to arrive, and given the odds against anyone qualifying, you might think that the Jewish community would enthusiastically, and en masse, welcome Jesus. But that wasn't the case. Except for a small ragtag group of followers, just about every segment of society was quick to reject Him as a viable candidate as the Messiah. It isn't that He failed to qualify; to the contrary, He satisfied all of the Messianic prophecies. His rejection was based on the fact that He wasn't the type of Messiah the people desired:

- The officials of the Roman Empire didn't really care about the religious affairs of the Jews. They wouldn't have minded a Messiah who restricted His influence solely to religious matters. But Jesus spoke of a kingdom of God to which the Jews should devote themselves. This put Jesus in direct competition with the emperor.

- The Jewish religious leaders had a sweet deal going. They lived an elevated and privileged lifestyle. They added hundreds of religious rules and then evaluated people based on their ability to keep the rules—an ability at which they themselves excelled. Jesus rocked them out of their complacency by exposing their hypocrisy and preaching the message that God didn't care about rules but was instead interested in heartfelt devotion.
- The general Jewish populace simply wanted relief from the oppression under which they lived. The wanted a heroic military Messiah who would vanquish the Roman Empire. The wanted a socially benevolent Messiah who would provide free food and other comforts of life.

Consider the amazing irony of all of this. God knew that the world needed a physical representation of Himself, so He came to earth as Jesus the God-Man. He appeared to the Jews, who were eager and desperate for a Messiah. He satisfied the profile of the prophesied Messiah in every detail, and they witnessed the miracles that Jesus performed. Yet their own prejudices and biases for their own self-interests caused them to reject Jesus as the one and true Messiah.

It would be easy for us to be critical of them for their astonishing short-sightedness, except that we often neglect to acknowledge the Lordship of Jesus Christ ourselves.

CHAPTER 27

···

THE KING NOBODY WANTED

He had no beauty or majesty to attract us to him,
nothing in his appearance that we should desire him.
He was despised and rejected by mankind,
a man of suffering, and familiar with pain.

ISAIAH 53:2–3

Kings these days don't have a very good reputation, mainly because they generally fall into one of two categories, neither of which carries much credibility with most people. Modern kings are either ceremonial and don't have any real authority, or they are dictators who rule with an iron fist. By comparison, kings in the Bible (such as Nebuchadnezzar, David, and Herod) were true monarchs, some good and some bad.

Unlike the imperfect and often tyrannical kings throughout history, Jesus was the perfect King. He had every right to rule over God's people. In fact, when Magi from the east came to Jerusalem to find Jesus, they asked King Herod, "Where is the one who has been born king of the Jews?" (Matthew 2:2). The question deeply troubled Herod, for he feared a competitor to his throne had been born. When the Magi double-crossed Herod, he furiously ordered the killing of every male child under the age of two to make sure this new king could never challenge him. Of course, Herod was dead wrong.

After an angel warned Jesus' parents of Herod's plan, they took Him and fled to Egypt, where they stayed until Herod died. The family then returned to the district of Galilee, to a town called Nazareth, where Jesus grew up as the son of a working-class carpenter, never once looking or acting like the King He was. He certainly didn't catch the attention of the local citizenry, who were oppressed by the Romans and always on the lookout for the Messiah the prophets had predicted. The Magi found the King they were looking for, but He wasn't the King the Jews were expecting. Jesus was born a commoner. They were looking for a conqueror capable of exerting political and military power to rescue them from their oppressors. So for thirty years, Jesus went unnoticed.

Then an eccentric prophet living in the wilderness announced to anyone who would listen (and some who wouldn't), "Repent, for the kingdom of heaven has come near" (Matthew 3:2). It was an overt clue that Jesus was indeed a King, but that His kingdom was not of this earth. Of course, Jesus knew what kind of King He was. While refusing any attempt by people around Him to make Him an earthly king (see John 6:15), Jesus echoed what John the Baptist had been saying: "Repent, for the kingdom of God has come near" (Matthew 4:17).

Three years later, Jesus stood before Pilate, the Roman governor of Palestine, as a man the religious leaders had accused of treason. Pilate summoned Jesus to his palace and interrogated Him. "Are you the king of the Jews?" he asked. Jesus defined the authority of His rule and reign when He replied, "My kingdom is not of this world."

Jesus was then beaten, mocked for His claim to kingship, and forced to carry a cross to Golgotha, where He was crucified as a common criminal beneath a sign that read, THIS IS JESUS, THE KING OF THE JEWS. The people didn't accept that title, of course, and even His close followers and friends all but deserted Him as He voluntarily died, bearing the sins of His executioners and of the whole world. But when He rose from the dead on the third day, ensuring that death had been conquered, God gave Jesus all kingly authority in heaven and on earth (see Matthew 28:18).

So why isn't Jesus literally ruling over the universe for all to see now? The answer is that King Jesus rules *over* us by ruling *within* us. Those who are part of His spiritual body, the church, are co-heirs of all the spiritual riches of God. We relate to Christ the King organically, not as subjects who bow to a monarch, but as a branch connected to and dependent upon the vine, deriving our spiritual life and nourishment from our Savior.

We live on earth under the authority of human rulers and governments, but we do so knowing that someday, perhaps soon or soon after we have left this earth, Jesus will return in power and great glory to reign. On that day, He will be acknowledged as "KING OF KINGS AND LORD OF LORDS" (Revelation 19:16), and every knee will bow and every tongue will confess that Jesus is the true King, worthy of all glory and honor:

> *Therefore God exalted him to the highest place*
> *and gave him the name that is above every name,*
> *that at that name of Jesus every knee should bow,*
> *in heaven and on earth and under the earth,*
> *and every tongue acknowledge that Jesus Christ*
> *is Lord, to the glory of God the Father.*
> PHILIPPIANS 2:9–11

CHAPTER 28

....

THE HERO EVERYBODY NEEDS

The heart of Christianity is a myth which is also a fact.
C. S. LEWIS

Everybody loves a hero. Whether it's a real-life, ordinary person who does something heroic in a moment of crisis, or a comic book superhero who saves the world from bad guys, we just love a good hero and a great heroic story. To say that Jesus was a hero might seem inappropriate, or even sacrilegious, because Jesus wasn't ordinary and He certainly didn't fly around in a cape. But if you give it some thought, it isn't all that far-fetched, especially when you consider the classic definition of a hero: "A being of godlike prowess and beneficence who often came to be honored as a divinity."

The idea of the classic hero has been a part of human lore, legend, and literature for thousands of years. Eight centuries before Jesus was born, the Greek poet Homer wrote two epic poems, *The Iliad* and *The Odyssey*, that defined the heroic tradition in literature. Odysseus, the hero of Homer's story, goes on a long journey following the fall of Troy in order to get home. But he doesn't get there until he experiences a series of adventures.

The American scholar Joseph Campbell developed this narrative pattern in a framework he called "The Hero's Journey." Used by writers, filmmakers, and storytellers, it describes the typical adventure of the hero in stages. The major ones are:

- The Call to Adventure
- Tests, Allies, and Enemies
- The Road of Trials
- Facing Death
- Resurrection
- Transforming the World

Many familiar stories use this framework. In fact, you could argue that *every* great story follows this pattern. That's why Campbell said they all were part of one great "monomyth," which is another way of saying "one story." But whose story is it? Did L. Frank Baum in *The Wizard of Oz* and J.R.R. Tolkien in *The Lord of the Rings* and the writers who told the story of Jesus in the Bible copy Homer, or are the elements of the Hero's journey embedded in the human consciousness?

Skeptics of the biblical narrative say the story of Jesus is simply a copy of other stories and myths. Just look how closely His story follows the framework of the Hero's Journey, they argue. But the great English scholar C.S. Lewis disagrees. (Yes, the author of *The Chronicles of Narnia,* another story that follows the pattern of the hero's journey, was a respected scholar.) Lewis contended that the reason these stories about heroes are common across cultures is because God has put them there. Lewis believed God has literally spoken to us through myth, and that He uses our familiarity with the monomyth—the one story—to make us comfortable with His Story.

One of the definitions of the word *myth* is "an invented story." If that's the case, then God's Story is a true myth, and Jesus is the true hero. Lewis referred to this as "myth became fact." In an essay by that name, he made the case that our acquaintance with myth brings us closer to the truth of reality. God has spoken to us through the parallels and similarities in morality and myth found in stories in every culture and in every historical era. The Myth that became Fact—the Incarnation, the tests, the relationships, the trials, the death and resurrection of Jesus—is the ultimate true myth that is more than a mere story. It is the Story that brings salvation and life to anyone who believes.

How amazing that God didn't just drop this story in our laps without any kind of innate and cultural familiarity. If He had, we would have trouble understanding. But God loves and cares about us too much to leave His dramatic, life-changing story to chance. He has opened the doors of our imaginations with stories told in the same familiar pattern, so that we can be receptive to the True Story that does much more than entertain us. This is the One Story that has the power to give us life.

CHAPTER 29

FULL OF INTELLIGENCE
AND WISDOM

*Socrates taught for forty years, Plato for fifty, Aristotle for forty,
and Jesus for only three. Yet the influence of Christ's three-year
ministry infinitely transcends the impact left by the combined
130 years of teaching from these men who were among the
greatest philosophers of all antiquity.*

UNKNOWN

Jesus was a teacher with a radical message. The hallmark of Christ's ministry was not the miracles He performed (those were only intended to provide proof that He was God's Son) but what He taught. His teaching was honest, fresh, and direct. He seemed to always be teaching, whether in crowds, around the dinner table, or one-on-one. People everywhere addressed Him as "Master" or "Rabbi," even though He never enrolled in rabbinical school.

Jesus was never boring when He spoke. Often what He said was controversial; occasionally it was confrontational; always it was insightful. In his Gospel, Mark reports that many "were amazed at his teaching, because he taught them as one who had authority" (Mark 1:22).

Working without cue cards or teleprompters, Jesus Christ was the world's greatest orator, teacher, and inspirational speaker. He always spoke God's truth, but He tailored His presentation to the audience and as a means of achieving an intended impact:

- Jesus frequently spoke in parables—using a common object or experience from daily life to illustrate a spiritual truth. For example, He used the story of a farmer planting seeds in four types of soil—roadside, rocky, weed-infested, and fertile—to illustrate how different people respond to God's message of new life (see Matthew 13:3–23).

- Sometimes Jesus would use an epigram—a short, wise statement, sometimes built around a paradox. Consider this unforgettable one: "Whoever finds their life will lose it, and whoever loses their life for my sake will find it" (Matthew 10:39).

- Jesus also effectively used questions. His rhetorical queries were usually mindbenders. For example, "What good will it be for someone to gain the whole world, yet forfeit their soul? Or what can anyone give in exchange for their soul?" (Matthew 16:26). His direct, personal questions were penetrating: "Who do people say I am? . . . Who do you say I am?" (Mark 8:27, 29).

- Jesus loved to use object lessons, illustrating His point with some familiar item or circumstance. For instance, when He noticed a widow contributing to the temple treasury, He took the opportunity to teach His disciples a lesson about sacrificial giving (see Luke 21:1–4).

Reading through the New Testament, we can see that Jesus was called by many names, such as Master, Lord, and Savior. But of the ninety times He was addressed directly in the Gospels, He was called "Teacher" on sixty of those occasions. This is the context in which Nicodemus approached Him: "We know that you are a teacher who has come from God" (John 3:2). This is what most crowds considered Him to be, and it is how He referred to Himself: "You call me 'Teacher' and 'Lord,' and rightly so, for that is what I am" (John 13:13).

In a culture in which rabbis quoted other rabbis, Jesus was a radical teacher because He spoke the authoritative words of God—and He could do that because He *was* God. When His teachings included quotes, they came directly from the God-inspired, sacred Scriptures, which to that point was what we know as the Old Testament. Otherwise, He was speaking God's truth.

Did Jesus' teaching have any lasting impact? Perhaps the best measure of His teaching success is to evaluate how His students promulgated His message. Remember that His final word to His followers was a command for them to teach what He had taught them:

> *"Therefore go and make disciples of all nations,*
> *baptizing them in the name of the Father and*
> *of the Son and of the Holy Spirit, and teaching*
> *them to obey everything I have commanded you."*
> MATTHEW 28:19–20

For three years, His disciples had been the recipients of His teaching. Were His methods effective enough for them to understand and absorb what He taught? Was His message impactful to the point where they would be motivated by it and dedicated to it, even in the face of tremendous opposition and adversity? The answer to these questions is not simply affirmative; it is amazing. In the words of author, speaker, and blogger Ray Pritchard:

> *How well did it work? Look around you.*
> *Two thousand years have passed and today across*
> *the world over two billion people bear his name.*
> *Christianity has spread from Jerusalem to every corner*
> *of the globe. At this very moment multiplied thousands*
> *of missionaries are doing what Jesus said to do: teaching*
> *all nations. If the success of the students is the measure*
> *of the teacher, then no teacher was ever so successful*
> *as the one and only Master Teacher, Jesus Christ.*

CHAPTER 30

....

THE ONE WHO
CALMED THE STORM

In the proper sense, a miracle is an event
which is not producible by the natural causes that are operative
in effect at the time and place the event occurs.
WILLIAM LANE CRAIG

Miracle is an overused word. Anything unexpected (or anything advertised on an infomercial) gets tagged as a miracle. So we end up with the "Miracle Mets" and a "Miracle Hair Remover." But the miracles of Jesus were more than unanticipated events or promotional hype. And they were more than astounding, unexplainable tricks.

Christ's miracles were supernatural acts that He caused outside of physical laws of the universe. Jesus wasn't just showing off. His miracles had specific purposes: to change human lives for the better and to prove that He was God. As the apostle John wrote, "What Jesus did here in Cana of Galilee [turning water into wine] was the first of the signs through which he revealed his glory; and his disciples believed in him" (John 2:11).

Christ's miracles can be categorized into three groups. His healing miracles proved His power over sickness and death (more about that in Chapter 31). A second group of miracles revealed His power over nature:

- He turned water into wine (John 2:1–11)
- He filled a net with fish (Luke 5:1–11)
- He calmed a storm (Mark 4:35–41)
- He fed more than five thousand people with five loaves and two fish (Matthew 14:13–21)
- He walked on water (Matthew 14:22–33)
- He fed another four thousand-plus people with seven loaves and several fish (Matthew 15:29–38)
- He filled a second net of fish (John 21:1–12)

And a third group of Christ's miracles proved His power over Satan and his demons:

- He delivered a man in the synagogue from demonic spirits (Mark 1:21–28)
- He cast out a dumb and blind spirit (Matthew 12:22–32)

- He cast out demons from a man at Gadara (Mark 5:1–20)
- He cast out a spirit from a mute man (Matthew 9:32–34)
- He cast demons out of a lunatic boy (Mark 9:14–29)

What you just read is likely only a partial list of the miracles Jesus performed. He probably performed many more miracles that were not recorded in Scripture. The disciple John indicated as much in the very last verse of his gospel: "Jesus did many other things as well. If every one of them were written down, I suppose that even the whole world would not have room for the books that would be written" (John 21:25).

The cumulative effect of these miracles should prompt a twofold response of faith and trust in Jesus Christ:

First, we should have a confidence that Jesus Christ was indeed God. He had a dual nature: all God and all man. (It's a God thing, so we can't fully comprehend it—but theologians refer to it as the "hypostatic union.") While Christ's occasional hunger and weariness reflect His humanity, the supernatural power to perform miracles reveals His divine nature.

Second, the miracles Christ performed should give us the faith and trust that He has the power to perform similar miracles in our lives if He chooses to do so. We are certain to encounter obstacles and challenges in our lives. Sometimes the circumstances of life stack up against us and we need divine intervention to find a way of relief; other times we may be the target of Satan's efforts. The Scripture confirms that our struggles may be against the "powers of this dark world and against the spiritual forces of evil in the heavenly realms" (Ephesians 6:12).

When you have storms in your life that seem overwhelming and you feel intimidated and helpless, remember this miracle reported in Mark 4:37–41:

> *A furious squall came up, and the waves broke over the boat, so that it was nearly swamped. Jesus was in the stern, sleeping on a cushion. The disciples woke him and said to him, "Teacher, don't you care if we drown?" He got up, rebuked the wind and said to the waves, "Quiet! Be still!" Then the wind died down and it was completely calm. He said to his disciples, "Why are you so afraid? Do you still have no faith?" They were terrified and asked each other, "Who is this? Even the wind and the waves obey him!"*

You too can put your faith in Jesus during the storms of life. You too will be amazed that His miraculous power can control the circumstances in your life for your safety and protection.

CHAPTER 31

....

FULL OF HEALING POWER

Each healing Jesus did was an eloquent sermon that made the point that He was Lord even over sickness and death. He told us to go and do likewise—to care for the poor and the sick. In two thousand years, millions of Christians have gone and done likewise.
D. JAMES KENNEDY

When the American woman first walked into the large home in Kolkata, India, the stench of death repulsed her. And if the offensive smells weren't bad enough, the moans and disgusting sounds were more than enough to send her scurrying away. But she had flown eight thousand miles from southern California to volunteer with the Missionaries of Charity, the relief organization established by Mother Teresa, and she had specifically chosen to be here, where fifty men and fifty women were in the final stages of death. So she busied herself with a project, hoping she could help without personally encountering any of the dying.

Then something caught her eye. From one side of the large room where she was working, a decrepit woman was waving her arm weakly, motioning for her to come. After a few moments of trying to avert her glance, the American reluctantly went over to the woman, who immediately began speaking to her with great emotion in a language she did not understand. Clearly the dying woman was in distress and wanted something from the American.

At that moment a feeling of deep compassion came over the American. She took the frail, dying figure into her arms and began to offer words of comfort and compassion, speaking English, but praying in the name of Jesus that God would be with her. "God loves you and cares about you," she said. "And He is here with you. I am embracing you with His arms and crying for you with His tears."

The American was Kay Warren, wife of the famous pastor and bestselling author Rick Warren. Her story, told at the commencement of a Christian university, illustrates the continuing power of Jesus to heal and show compassion to the suffering, the marginalized, the hopeless, and the dying.

Early in His public ministry, Jesus made it clear why He came to live in this imperfect world. Responding to His critics, who asked why He ate with "tax collectors and sinners," Jesus said, "It is not the healthy who need a doctor, but the sick. I have not come to call the righteous, but sinners" (Mark 2:17).

Jesus is known as the Great Physician, and even among unbelievers He is perceived as a healer of the sick. Not only did He have the *power* to heal, cast out demons, and raise the dead, but He had the *authority* as well. Jesus didn't just heal because people were sick; He healed in response to faith. Once a woman who had been "subject to bleeding" for twelve years came up behind Jesus and touched His cloak, believing she would be healed without making any physical contact. The Bible tells us, "Immediately her bleeding stopped and she felt in her body that she was free from her suffering." When Jesus realized what had happened, He said to her, "Daughter, your faith has healed you. Go in peace and be freed from your suffering" (see Mark 5:25–34).

In this statement, Jesus was saying that His healing is both physical and spiritual. In fact, the Greek word for "healed" also means "saved."

There's not a person with faith in Jesus who doubts that He can heal people physically, even today. When we pray in the name of Jesus for someone who is suffering, we expect physical healing. But we also know that people with faith don't always get well, and we wonder why not. Only God knows, and His purposes for us aren't always clear at the time we are going through difficulty. What we do know, however, is that Jesus always heals spiritually. His healing power to alleviate suffering, which is temporary, as well as to bring peace to the soul, which is eternal, comes from the same supernatural source.

That's why Kay Warren's story is so powerful. The woman in the Mother Teresa home for the dying was not restored physically, but she was blessed and healed spiritually. Like Kay, we need to be the arms and tears of Jesus to the sick and dying, and we need to think in spiritual terms, not just physical. God may not use us to heal someone in the physical sense, but He can certainly use us in amazing ways to help people heal spiritually.

CHAPTER 32

···

FULL OF COMPASSION

*The character of Jesus has not only been the highest pattern
of virtue, but the strongest incentive in its practice, and has
exerted so deep an influence, that it may be truly said that the
simple record of three short years of active life has done more to
regenerate and to soften mankind than all the disquisitions of
philosophers and all the exhortations of moralists.*
W.E. LECKY

Forget the artists' depiction of Jesus that make Him
look skinny, pale, and effeminate. Reject the notion
that He tromped up and down the dusty roads around
Galilee for three years and never got any dirt on His
white robe with the blue satin sash. And He didn't
have a delicate halo hovering over His head, either.

In stark contrast to popular images, Jesus was a
rugged man's man. His closest friends were men who
worked on commercial fishing boats for a living. Jesus

made a commando-style raid on shady businessmen in the temple courtyard. He got in the faces of hypocritical religious leaders and called them a "brood of vipers" and "white-washed graves." Rather than leading a docile and timid existence, Jesus was assertive to the point of triggering death threats.

Yet His ruggedness didn't prevent Him from being compassionate toward women, children, the poor, and the sick or disabled. It was this side of His personality that was a radical departure from the cultural norms.

It is important for us to remember that the world Jesus was born into was a cruel place. Disease and deformity were common. The Roman government—in power throughout Christ's time on earth—was a formidable political power with benefits that flowed to its citizens. But if you were not a Roman citizen and were in need, you had virtually no chance of receiving help. To make matters worse, if you were a woman or a child, you were less than a second-class member of society. If you were a slave (and there were six million slaves in the Roman world at that time), you were someone else's property. If you had a disease, you were ostracized from society.

Into this cultural setting and mind-set, Jesus appears on the scene, embodying a message of compassion and justice. He challenged and undermined all of the barriers between the rich and the poor, between the free and the slave, and between the healthy and the infirm. He instigated a cultural revolution, but it wasn't accomplished by brute force. He did it simply by setting an example for others to follow.

Disregarding social conventions, Jesus personally mingled with society's outcasts and touched those considered untouchable. He wasn't just sympathetic toward people's suffering. Sympathy is merely an emotion or sorrow for someone who endures misfortune. As the apostle Paul stated in 2 Corinthians 1:3, Jesus was full of "compassion," which combines the emotion of sympathy with definite action taken to alleviate suffering. His compassion caused Him to have a heart for the disadvantaged and motivated Him to do something about it. So He healed the sick, gave food to the hungry, and comforted those who were exploited.

When He was caring for the needs of the poor, the afflicted, and the oppressed, Jesus was instructing His followers to do so by example. In one of His best-known parables, the story of the Good Samaritan, He taught the importance of helping anyone who is in need—whether the person is a friend, stranger, or enemy. In His "Sermon on the Mount," He taught that God did not favor the rich and powerful because of their position and prestige. To the contrary, He held that God's blessings were reserved for those who mourn, those who are hungry and thirsty for justice, and for those who are persecuted because they live for God (see Matthew 5:3–10).

Jesus ascribed dignity and importance to helping the disadvantaged, and He identified with them. Matthew 25 recounts His explanation that when we feed the hungry, give clothing to the poor, extend hospitality to strangers, care for those who are sick, and visit the imprisoned, it is as if we are doing these things for Jesus Himself. Jesus legitimized the radical notion that there are no expendable members of society and that God loves the disadvantaged.

Amazingly, Christ's display of compassion began a culture-shift in the first century. A spirit of compassion germinated within those early Christians, and they willingly shared their possessions with others to fend off poverty. They distributed food in the care of widows.

Twenty centuries later, organizations founded on Christ's principles—such as the Salvation Army, World Vision, Habitat for Humanity, and Compassion International—are giving aid and comfort to millions of people in hundreds of countries. It all began with Christ's "show and tell" of going beyond sympathy to a point of compassion.

CHAPTER 33

....

ABLE TO FORGIVE

You cannot forgive a debt without taking it on yourself.
TIM KELLER

It was a hot night, and the little house owned by the impulsive Peter, one of Jesus' disciples, was full of people. Jesus was in the middle of the curious crowd, most of whom were there to see if the man from Galilee would be doing any healing or performing miracles of any kind.

Lately, Jesus' healing ministry had attracted thousands of people. So crushing were the crowds that He could "no longer enter a town openly but stayed outside in lonely places" (Mark 1:45). Jesus snuck into the town where Peter lived, perhaps to rest and recover, but the people heard He was there and jammed into the house where He was staying. Jesus knew what the fickle crowd wanted, but He stayed true to His mission and "preached the word to them" (Mark 2:2).

As Jesus was preaching, a commotion came from above. Since there was no room for them in the house, some men had carried a friend, a paralyzed man, onto the roof, hoping to gain access to Jesus. To the amazement of the crowd below, the men tore an opening in the roof and lowered their friend on a mat until he was right in front of Jesus. He looked at the paralyzed man before Him, and then looked up at the men who were peering through the hole they had made. Rather than viewing them as disrupters, Jesus saw them as people of great faith, and it moved Him. Looking at the paralyzed man, Jesus said, "Son, your sins are forgiven" (Mark 2:5).

There were some Pharisees in the room, experts in the Law who constantly hounded and harassed Jesus, and when they heard His words, they immediately accused Him of blasphemy. "Who can forgive sins but God alone?" they said indignantly.

With that question, these critics of Jesus demonstrated that they understood the amazing implications of what Jesus had just done. As dramatic as the physical tableau in the house appeared to be, the Pharisees recognized the unspoken meaning of what Jesus had just said, and they weren't about to let Him get away with it. Jesus knew what was in their hearts, and He called them on it. "Why are you thinking these things?" He asked them. "Which is easier: to say to this paralyzed man, 'Your sins are forgiven,' or to say, 'Get up, take your mat and walk'? But I want you to know that the Son of Man has authority on earth to forgive sins" (see Mark 2:8–10).

In that dramatic moment, Jesus claimed that He was equal to God, and the Pharisees knew it. They knew from the prophets that it is God who "blots out your transgressions" (Isaiah 43:25). What they didn't know, but were finding out in vivid detail, is that Jesus, the Creator of the universe, God in human form, makes it possible.

In his book *Encounters with Jesus,* Tim Keller engages the reader in a thought experiment to illustrate the true nature of forgiveness. What if someone were to knock over your lamp and break it? She would likely apologize and offer to pay for it, which leaves you with two choices. You can either thank her and make her pay, or you can forgive her and tell her it's not necessary. Regardless of what you do, you still have to deal with the lamp. Either you or your friend has to pay for a replacement, or you have to go without a lamp. "In other words," writes Keller, "either that person pays or you pay. The debt doesn't vanish."

This hypothetical situation illustrates God's nature and the way He forgives. As a holy God, He can't just look down on our debt, which is our sin and the way we treat each other and the world He created, and say, "I forgive you, so I'll give you a pass on your debt." There's still a debt to pay, just like there's a lamp to replace, even though forgiveness has been offered. Keller points out that God's insistence that our debt is paid is not because He doesn't love us enough. "Actually, it's quite the opposite," Keller continues. "God is so holy that he had to come in the form of Jesus Christ and die to pay the debt, but he is so loving he was glad to come and die for you."

So when Jesus forgave the sins of the paralyzed man, much to the horror of the Pharisees, it was because God alone can forgive sin, which He does through the person and finished work of Jesus Christ on the cross. All the sins of all people who will ever believe in Jesus, including that paralyzed man, including you, were placed on Christ on that cross, thereby paying the debt and satisfying the holiness and justice of God.

The beautiful words of the hymn writer Charles Wesley express our wonder at this glorious thought:

Amazing love! How can it be
that thou my God should die for me?

CHAPTER 34

....

THE ONE WHO
SUFFERED AND DIED

*Men have said that the cross of Christ was not a heroic thing,
but I want to tell you that the cross of Jesus Christ has put more
heroism in the souls of men than any other event in human history.*
JOHN G. LAKE

We've heard it so often that, sadly, it has become mundane and trite. We tend to ignore the cosmic consequences of the story. If Jesus Christ were only a man, then the storyline would hardly be unusual enough to make it newsworthy:

- After three years of public ministry as an itinerant preacher, Jesus headed to Jerusalem for what will be the final journey of His earthly ministry.

- As He entered the city, a huge following started to celebrate Him as some sort of religious superstar.

- Recognizing Christ's popularity and seeing it as a threat, religious leaders plotted to put Jesus to death. After all, Jesus could jeopardize their system of rules and regulations and the hierarchy they wanted to protect. Jesus taught that the condition of a person's heart for God was more important than religious rituals. If the people believed this, then the job security of the religious establishment was endangered.

- With the help of one of His own disciples, Christ's enemies arrested Him. The charges were phony, and the traitor was paid a bounty. Conspiring with the Roman governor, the religious elite ran Jesus through a series of kangaroo courts, each one a sham. The fabricated evidence violated procedural laws.

- Based on the trumped-charges and the crooked court system, Jesus' antagonists succeeded in obtaining both a guilty verdict and a death sentence. Although several means of execution were available, they chose crucifixion—the most painful and tortuous method, reserved for the most heinous offenders.

- As the falsely accused protagonist hung on the cross for about three hours, there were some atmospheric theatrics. Otherwise, everything was rather routine, and the lifeless body was taken down and placed in a tomb.

But Jesus Christ was not only a man. He was God incarnate, and that is what makes the story so amazing:

- Satan thought this entire scenario was playing out exactly according to his plan for Christ's annihilation. But he was sorely mistaken. In actuality, these events were playing out exactly according to God's own secret plan—whereby salvation would be available to all of humanity—which He had decided on long before the creation of the universe.

- As omnipotent God, Jesus could have brought an army of angels to His defense. He was not helpless in any respect. He voluntarily went to Calvary; it was His choice to endure the pain and torture of crucifixion. His love for each and every one of us motivated Him.

- Christ's motivating love is greater than we can imagine. Not one of us was lovable. At the time He died for us, we were sinners. That is a big deal for a holy God. To Him, our sins are filthy and detestable. In God's paradigm, our sin makes a relationship with Him impossible and makes us deserving of eternal death.

- But in His grace, God extends His love to us (which we don't deserve), and His mercy spares us from eternal death (which we do deserve). At the very moment when our sins made us God's enemies, God permitted His sinless Son to be tortured to death so that the judgment for our sin could be satisfied.

This was not ordinary, routine, run-of-the-mill execution. The central character was the One True God. Thus, it had eternal ramifications for every member of the human race. But what makes these events incomprehensible is the extent of God's love.

At the end of the immediately preceding chapter, we quoted a line from a Charles Wesley hymn. Here are more lines from the same hymn that aptly express the wonder that overwhelms us as we consider God's love, which caused Christ to hang on the Cross in our place:

And can it be that I should gain
An interest in the Savior's blood?
Died He for me, who caused His pain?
For me, who Him to death pursued?
Amazing love! How can it be
That Thou, my God, should die for me?

He left His Father's throne above
(So free, so infinite His grace!),
Emptied Himself of all but love,
And bled for Adam's helpless race:
'Tis mercy all, immense and free,
For O my God, it found out me!

No condemnation now I dread;
Jesus, and all in Him, is mine!
Alive in Him, my living Head,
And clothed in righteousness divine,
Bold I approach th'eternal throne,
And claim the crown, through Christ my own.

CHAPTER 35

....

THE ONE WHO
CONQUERED DEATH

The early Christians did not invent the empty tomb and the meetings of sightings of the risen Jesus. . . . To suggest otherwise is to stop doing history and enter into a fantasy world of our own.
N.T. WRIGHT

The resurrection of Jesus Christ has been and continues to be one of history's most hotly contested events. Because it contains the words *history* and *event*, that sentence alone would probably infuriate any number of people groups: atheists, agnostics, skeptics, and naturalists, not to mention members of the world's other two great monotheistic religions—Islam and Judaism. Both believe Jesus was a real person, and Islam even calls Him a prophet, but devout followers in both camps would agree with the atheists and skeptics that the resurrection of Jesus is myth, not fact.

That leaves Christians as the one people group who *should* accept the Resurrection as true, but that's not necessarily the way it is. Not every follower of Christ believes He is alive right now in His resurrected body, sitting at the right hand of God the Father (see Romans 8:34). For a growing number of people, those kinds of details aren't important. To them, it's all about loving God and loving people. As we heard someone say recently, "If you get those two things right, nothing else matters."

It's true that Jesus said all the commandments could be summarized in this one "greatest commandment" (see Matthew 22:37–38), but there are some other things that matter, such as the reality of the resurrection of Jesus from the dead. In fact, according to the apostle Paul, if the resurrection of Jesus did not happen, our faith is futile, and we are still in our sins. "If only for this life we have hope in Christ," Paul writes, "we are of all people most to be pitied" (1 Corinthians 15:19).

But history shows the Resurrection did happen. As Timothy Keller points out, "The resurrection of Jesus is a historical fact much more fully attested to than most other events of ancient history we take for granted."

So why do people, including some Christians, doubt that it happened? Actually, doubts about the Resurrection have been around since the day it happened, when Roman soldiers hired to guard Jesus' tomb were ambushed by an angel from heaven who rolled the stone away from the mouth of the grave. Sheepishly, the guards went to Jerusalem to report to their employers, the chief priests and the Pharisees, on the now-empty tomb. The religious leaders then conferred and came up with a plan that would discredit the resurrection story now spreading like wildfire. They decided to offer the Roman military guard "a large sum of money" to tell everyone that the disciples of Jesus had snuck in at night and stolen the body so they could say Jesus was risen.

There was only one problem: eyewitness accounts of the living Christ contradicted the made-up story. And it wasn't just the friends and followers of Jesus who saw Him. The apostle Paul writes that Jesus appeared to "more than five hundred" people at the same time (see 1 Corinthians 15:6). Still, the story of the stolen body persisted until Matthew wrote his Gospel a good twenty-five years after the miraculous event took place.

And of course, we know the story is still circulated today, because, frankly, the idea of an amazing, supernatural event like the resurrection of Jesus makes many people uncomfortable. We can understand that—to a point. Miracles aren't easy to get your mind around, and they are impossible to prove using scientific methods. So we have to grant some latitude when it comes to believing miraculous events. People need a little space and time to consider the evidence for the Resurrection.

But it's critical to come to a place of belief in this miraculous event—because it really happened.

Those who continue to deny the Resurrection are by implication stripping Jesus of His deity, which means they are left with nothing more than a great dead moral teacher, like Buddha or Muhammad. As C.S. Lewis famously pointed out in his "Liar, Lunatic, or Lord" trilemma, Jesus doesn't allow for the great moral teacher option. He claimed in no uncertain terms to be God (see John 8:58–59 and 10:30 for starters), and the Resurrection has been corroborated as an historical fact. If either of those claims is anything less than absolutely true, then you have a self-deluded Jesus (or worse) and a Bible that can't be trusted.

Perhaps there's a bigger reason why many people, including some who would still claim to be followers of Jesus, deny or at the very least doubt the Resurrection. If Jesus is alive and sitting at the right hand of the Father, then He is equal to God in every way. And that means we are responsible to Him, both in our lives here on earth and in the life to come.

We are still free to live life on our own terms, but Jesus has shown us a better life, an amazing life. And in the end it is the only life that matters.

CHAPTER 36

....

IN HEAVEN WORKING
ON OUR BEHALF

Jesus came into this world immaculately, lived extraordinarily,
died excruciatingly, rose victoriously and ascended gloriously back
into Heaven, promising to one day return and take us home.
JASON JOHNSON

Once people have achieved their "purpose in life,"
their tendency is to coast through the rest of their days
and enjoy the benefits of their accomplishments. This
doesn't mean they will be lazy for the remainder of
their lifetimes. But the heavy lifting is over. Life can be
lived at a more enjoyable pace.

Politics provides the perfect example of this:
once a person has served as president of the United
States, he or she is not likely to run for the office of
hometown mayor. The daily grind of political office
is set aside for more tranquil and high-paying stints as

a keynote speaker and a board member for charitable foundations.

What about Jesus Christ? It has been approximately two thousand years since the crucifixion and resurrection. The Bible says that Christ will return to earth, but that future date is known only to God. No one would criticize Jesus if He decided to take a couple of centuries off for a well-deserved rest. But that is not what He is doing. The love that drove Him to the cross to pay for our salvation is not the extent of His work on our behalf. On the contrary, He has remained fully engaged and active for our benefit.

After making the ultimate sacrifice for us, Christ ascended to heaven, where He was glorified and given the place of honor He deserves: sitting at the right hand of our heavenly Father:

> *That power is the same as the mighty strength he [God the Father] exerted when he raised Christ from the dead and seated him at his right hand in the heavenly realms, far above all rule and authority, power and dominion, and every name that is invoked, not only in the present age but also in the one to come.*
> EPHESIANS 1:19–21

From this position of authority, Christ rules over all of creation. As He has been since eternity past, Christ is all-powerful, all-knowing, and everywhere present. We can live with the confident knowledge that He remains in charge of the universe in which we reside. He holds the world together, so we know He is able to deal with any challenge or stress we may encounter:

The Son is the image of the invisible God, the firstborn over all creation. For in him all things were created: things in heaven and on earth, visible and invisible, whether thrones or powers or rulers or authorities; all things have been created through him and for him. He is before all things, and in him all things hold together.
COLOSSIANS 1:15–17

Christ is also active in His role of High Priest who intercedes on our behalf. While His work on the cross was complete for our salvation, He plays an integral role in our relationship with God the Father:

Because Jesus lives forever, he has a permanent priesthood. Therefore he is able to save completely those who come to God through him, because he always lives to intercede for them. Such a high priest truly meets our need—one who is holy, blameless, pure, set apart from sinners, exalted above the heavens.
HEBREWS 7:24–26

As our High Priest, Jesus intercedes for us with God. He brings our prayers and petitions before God on our behalf. Together they confer about what is best for us—what we need and don't need—and work all things together for our good so that we may become mature in our faith and reflect the nature of Christ.

And Christ is our Advocate. Even though salvation is secure for all believers, Satan is a great accuser and persists in pointing out our faults and failures to God. But Christ is our great Defender. He stands before

God as an eternal reminder of the righteousness we have obtained through Him.

> *My dear children, I write this to you so that you will not sin. But if anybody does sin, we have an advocate with the Father—Jesus Christ, the Righteous One. He is the atoning sacrifice for our sins, and not only for ours but also for the sins of the whole world.*
> 1 JOHN 2:1–2

Christ is also engaged in making heaven ready for our arrival. All believers were included in the encouragement He gave His disciples about the assurance of His return and our eventual residence in heaven:

> *"Do not let your hearts be troubled. You believe in God; believe also in me. My Father's house has many rooms; if that were not so, would I have told you that I am going there to prepare a place for you? And if I go and prepare a place for you, I will come back and take you to be with me that you also may be where I am."*
> JOHN 14:1–3

It is entirely appropriate that we focus on the amazing work Christ did for us in the past when He died sacrificially on the cross. But let's not forget what Christ is doing for us right now. He is at work in heaven on our behalf. The work He is doing sustains us, protects us, and makes future provision for us. Death on the cross was not enough. Christ continues to do more for you. His love for you is truly amazing.

PART 4

AMAZING GRACE

INTRODUCTION

....

He giveth more grace as our burdens grow greater,
He sendeth more strength as our labors increase;
To added afflictions He addeth His mercy,
To multiplied trials He multiplies peace.
ANNIE J. FLINT

We love *Star Wars,* and we can't wait for the next series
of movies based on the remarkable story that takes
place "a long time ago in a galaxy far, far away." George
Lucas brought fantasy and wonder back to the silver
screen and to the collective consciousness of millions
of fans, but he also distorted the reality of God. In
Lucas's worldview, there is a higher power, but it is
an impersonal "force" that can provide guidance when
called upon but otherwise stays in the background.

As a consequence, a lot of people believe that
God is nothing more than an impersonal force or an
absent deity who is out there somewhere in space but
doesn't much get involved in our daily affairs. How

utterly false! Not only is our amazing God active in our world, but He also delights in being involved in every detail of our lives (see Psalm 37:23). And because of His amazing characteristics, His incredible creative power, and the awesomeness of Jesus, we have an open invitation to join God as He continues on His mission to redeem a broken world. It is by grace that we are invited into a relationship with Him, and it is by grace that we live as His representatives in our neighborhoods and communities and beyond, helping to make them better places even as we long for the ultimate prize of knowing Him fully.

In the space of just three chapters in his second letter to the Corinthian church, the apostle Paul describes us as "*the pleasing aroma of Christ* among those who are being saved and those who are perishing" (2:15, italics added); "*a letter from Christ. . .*written not with ink but with the Spirit of the living God, not on tablets of stone but on tablets of human hearts" (3:3, italics added); and "*Christ's ambassadors*, as though God were making his appeal through us" (5:20, italics added).

All of these metaphors indicate that we are representatives and reflections of God's amazing grace in the world. What an enormous privilege! We hope the following chapters will inspire you to let God's grace pour through you on a daily basis as you encounter people who are desperate to experience God and His amazing grace.

Chapter 37

....

What God Requires of You

God's definition of what matters is pretty straightforward.
He measures our lives by how we love.
Francis Chan

There is a basic question that can be asked of every religion: "What is required to 'get in'?" Oftentimes there is a long list of preconditions people must satisfy. You've got to *stop* doing certain things, and you must *begin* doing other things. You have to clean up your act and promise to be something different than you currently are. In other words, you have to work for it, and you are judged on your performance.

Not so with Christianity. It is simply amazing that the entrance requirements for Christianity are so simple. To follow Jesus, you can "come as you are." No lifestyle overhaul is required. How can it be so simple? Because your salvation is not based on anything you have done—or anything you promise to do in the future:

God saved you by his grace when you believed. And you can't take credit for this; it is a gift from God. Salvation is not a reward for the good things we have done, so none of us can boast about it. For we are God's masterpiece. He has created us anew in Christ Jesus, so we can do the good things he planned for us long ago.
Ephesians 2:8–10 nlt

Here's the beautiful thing about all this: God loves you for who you are. You don't have to perform for God in order to win His favor. The beauty and wonder of your life in Christ is that your initial and continuing connection with God is not dependent upon your conduct. *There is nothing you can do to make God love you more* (so you don't have to perform for Him like some trained circus monkey). *And, there is nothing you can do to make God love you less* (so you don't have to fret about the screw-ups you will inevitably make). All you have to do to begin your new life in Christ is to believe and receive the free gift of salvation He offers you.

But what about all those Commandments people talk so much about—all those "Thou shalt not's"? First of all, God doesn't require adherence to any commandments as a prerequisite for your salvation. Remember that God rescued the Israelites from slavery in Egypt *before* He gave them the Ten Commandments.

God didn't make all those Jews memorize and comply with Commandments 1 through 10 as a precondition to sending the plagues on Pharaoh. Instead, He *rescued them first* and proclaimed them to be His children, *and then* He presented the Ten Commandments to show them what life looks like for devoted followers of God.

And the same principles are applicable to us in the twenty-first century. God rescued us from the slavery of sin while we were still slaves to it. Now that we have freedom in Christ, there is a suitable lifestyle for those who are truly grateful for the love God has demonstrated toward us. It is not an issue of what is *required* for us to do—again, remember that we aren't graded on our performance. Rather, it is a question of what is appropriate for us as followers of Christ.

Jesus summed it up in a conversation He had with a smart-alecky lawyer. Matthew 22:35–40 reports it this way:

Lawyer:	Teacher, what is the greatest commandment in the law?
Jesus:	"Love the Lord your God with all your heart and with all your soul and with all your mind." This is the first and greatest commandment. And the second is like it: "Love your neighbor as yourself." All the Law and the Prophets hang on these two commandments.

If you are looking for what it takes to be a Christian, that's it. Love God and love others. It is simply stated, but the ramifications are deep. A genuine love for God will motivate you to communicate with Him through reading the Bible and prayer; you'll have the desire to worship Him through service to others. Loving others won't always necessarily be easy or come naturally (as you may already know people who aren't easy to love), but that will be your natural response to the God you love. You need not do it out of compulsion, guilt, or fear. It will be the instinctive reaction of your heart. God doesn't want love from you that is coerced. His love for you is so amazing that, once you accept and understand it, it generates wholehearted devotion in return.

And that's what God wants to receive from you.

CHAPTER 38

....

GOD LOVES UNDERDOGS

*Though the world may be tilted toward the rich
and powerful, God is tilted toward the underdog.*
PHILIP YANCEY

Everybody loves underdogs, but nobody wants to be one. Our tendency is to want to be on top, to win, to achieve, and to have a minimal number of setbacks. Few of us us would say, "Before I get my next degree/job/sale/promotion/raise/relationship, I'd like to fail first." Not us. But failure happens, doesn't it? Few of us have gotten where we are without playing the role of underdog a few times.

No doubt you've been in that position before, and you've been amazed at how people get behind you. They want you to succeed. And when you finally do achieve that goal that cost you something, everyone is thrilled for you.

The same principle apples when it comes to rooting for another person. Whether you're watching a friend, your spouse or child, or even a complete stranger who happens to be the underdog, you get behind them. If a "Cinderella" team emerges in sports, everybody starts pulling for them to win. It's in our natures to love underdogs.

We have a theory about why we love underdogs. We love them because God loves them. In fact, as you read through the Bible and take notes on the kind of men and women God uses, you basically come up with an Underdog Hall of Fame. Here are some of our favorites:

- **Noah**: He was the laughingstock of the neighborhood for building something no one could figure out in order to save his family before something no one had ever seen destroyed the world. Yet that's exactly what he did.
- **Abraham and Sarah**: In a culture that placed great value on a large family, this couple was childless well into their eighties. Against all odds, God gave them a son and made Abraham the father of a great nation.
- **Jacob**: This underdog was a deceiver (his name means "crooked") and, true to his name, he cheated his brother out of his birthright. Yet God trusted him and made him the father of twelve sons who become the patriarchs of

the twelve tribes of Israel.

- **Joseph**: Though his jealous brothers sold him into slavery, and then he was falsely accused and put in prison, Joseph was a man God eventually elevated to second in command in Egypt and used to save the people of Israel during a great famine.
- **Moses**: He killed an Egyptian and fled to Midian, yet God restored this "friend of God" and used him to lead the God's people out of slavery in Egypt.
- **Rahab**: She was a prostitute who protected two spies on a mission from God from the enemy. Rahab was later spared and eventually appeared in the genealogy of Jesus.
- **David**: The youth who would become Israel's greatest monarch was the runt of the litter and too young to have any military experience, but God enabled him to defeat Goliath and become a great king.
- **Mary and Elizabeth**: The young virgin named Mary had to endure the gossip and derision of others because of her unexplained pregnancy. Her cousin Elizabeth was barren, yet she gave birth to a prophet who would announce the coming of Mary's child, Jesus the Messiah.
- **The twelve apostles**: These men were from the lower levels of society and had been passed over for any kind of prestigious religious positions, yet Jesus called them to something

greater and inspired them to change the world.

- **Paul**: Jesus personally called this one-time Jewish persecutor of the early Christians to be a witness to the Gentiles.

And then there's Jesus, who came from very humble beginnings and never ventured more than two hundred miles from His birthplace. He owned very little, never had a home to call His own, had nothing we would associate with power and influence, and was constantly opposed by the very people He came to save. Yet He has become the most influential person in human history and has more followers than any other person the world has ever known.

By the world's standards, all of these "heroes of the faith" started out as underdogs. If that's where you are right now, be grateful for your position and don't try to fight your way out on your own terms. That's a sure way to end up frustrated and defeated. Surrender to God and let Him take control.

"Our God loves doing things on our behalf," writes A. W. Tozer. "He loves it when we humble ourselves."

God loves underdogs.

CHAPTER 39

....

GOD WANTS TO USE
YOUR FAILURES

Our problem isn't that we've failed. Our problem is that we haven't failed enough. We haven't been brought low enough to learn what God wants us to learn.
CHUCK SWINDOLL

You can't avoid failure, and it's really pointless to try. You can do everything in your power to keep from failing, but you'll never succeed 100 percent of the time. And that's a good thing, because God only uses failures. To put it another way, if you don't fail, God won't use you. It is as simple as that.

This doesn't mean you should deliberately put yourself in situations where you know you will fail, just so God can teach you a valuable lesson. To the best of your ability, you need to put yourself in positions where you can succeed. But you must realize that *despite your best efforts and through no fault of your own*, failure is sometimes going to happen.

Failure hurts, but you can't let it get you down, because failure puts you in a place where God can use you. Amazingly, God uses your failures as part of His plan for you to be successful.

Other times, failure will come upon you *because you acted improperly or because you didn't take required action*. Maybe you did the opposite of what should have been done. Perhaps you lied when you should have been truthful, said something hateful about someone to make yourself look good, or intentionally overlooked an opportunity to help someone in a time of need. In such circumstances, you need to recognize your mistake, confess your sin, and accept God's forgiveness. It will hurt; but again, you will be positioned for God to bring about good through you.

The Bible is replete with accounts of people God used in great ways, and after they had failed in some colossal manner. Their failure was the tipping point at which God could begin to use them in ways no one could have predicted:

- Adam and Eve disobeyed God and brought sin and death upon the entire human race—which must rank fairly high on the list of World's Greatest Failures. Yet God used their disaster to introduce His plan of salvation through Jesus Christ (see Romans 5:18).

- Moses committed murder and fled to the obscurity of the wilderness. Yet God used him to lead the Jews out of slavery in Egypt (see Exodus 3:10).
- David made a series of bad decisions—resulting in adultery and murder—that nearly destroyed his kingdom, yet the Lord forgave him and arranged that the Messiah would be born from "the line of David" (see Luke 1:31–33).
- Elijah got depressed and wallowed in self-pity. This is the point at which God strengthened and cared for him (see 1 Kings 19:4, 7, 12).
- Peter denied Christ but was still useful to God. For that reason, he stands as an example of how you should never assume that your failings are fatal (see John 21:15–22).
- The apostle Paul struggled with sin, even though he knew better. Yet through Jesus Christ he could claim victory over sin (see Romans 7:24–25).

Do you see the pattern here? Every person God uses has a history of failure. Incredibly, God actually uses failure to accomplish His purposes. So rather than becoming discouraged when you fall short, see your failures as opportunities. Rather than living your life under the fear of failure, go through each day with the confidence Paul encourages you to have in Romans 8:28 (NLT): "And we know that God causes all things to work together for the good of those who love God and are called according to his purpose for them."

To experience the wonder of God's power to work through your failure, learn to see it from God's viewpoint. On the one hand we need to view sin as something God hates. On the other, from God's perspective, your failure might bring to you a sense of humility and dependence upon Him that helps you mature in your faith.

As far your failure is concerned:

- *God expects it.* He isn't a cynic, but a realist. Our failures don't surprise Him because He know our weaknesses.
- *God forgives it.* There's nothing you can do that God can't forgive.
- *God sees past it.* Your failures don't discourage, dishearten, or disillusion God.
- *God uses it.* God is a master of taking something weak and useless and using it for His purposes and glory.

God is in the business of transforming those He loves into something better—into persons who become more and more Christlike. Isn't it amazing that He can use our failures for that purpose?

CHAPTER 40

....

GOD IS FOR THE WEAK

But he said to me, "My grace is sufficient for you,
for my power is made perfect in weakness."
THE APOSTLE PAUL
2 CORINTHIANS 12:9

In many ways the Christian faith, which is based on the person and work of Jesus, is upside down—that is, if you view it from the world's perspective. Culture tells you to hate your enemies, but Jesus tells you to "love your enemies and pray for those who persecute you" (Matthew 5:44). The world advises you to get revenge if you have been wronged, but Jesus says, "If anyone slaps you on the right cheek, turn to them the other cheek also" (Matthew 5:39). We naturally hire lawyers to defend us in a lawsuit, but Jesus advises, "If anyone wants to sue you and take your shirt, hand over your coat as well" (Matthew 5:40).

If you were to actually do what Jesus says, how do you think others would react? They would probably think you are weak, and that's the last image any of us wants to project. Nobody likes to be called *weak*. Weakness is what sick people or cowards have, not those who are healthy and strong. That's why we do everything we can to avoid appearing weak. Yet that's exactly what God wants us to be. We know, it sounds crazy—but you're going to be amazed when we tell you why.

God prefers weakness over strength. That seems counterintuitive, but He's got a very good reason for it: when we are weak, God's power is made perfect. Our tendency is to exercise our rights, protect our reputation, and flex our muscles. But God tells us to let *Him* do the heavy lifting, let Him worry about our rights, let Him protect us, and let Him be strong for us.

And it's not just because He's better at this stuff than we are. The problem with fighting our own battles is that we never win, even when it looks like we did. When we conquer our enemies, get revenge, or win the lawsuit—and we think we've done it through our own wits and in our own power—our hearts tend to drift away from God. After all, why do we need Him when we can do it ourselves?

The problem is that we can't keep it up forever. At some point, we are going to lose, and lose badly—and then we'll come crawling to God, pleading for Him to help us. And in His graciousness and love, He will help us. But by then, the damage has been done. That's why God asks us to trust Him in the first place, not as an afterthought.

When David faced Goliath, a seasoned, well-armored, and very large soldier, the teenager took him down with a sling shot. There was no earthly reason why this shepherd boy was able to defeat such an enemy, but David knew how he had done it. He told the crowd looking on as he faced his enemy, "All those gathered here will know that it is not by sword or spear that the LORD saves; for the battle is the LORD's" (1 Samuel 17:47).

When Gideon brought an army of thirty-two thousand to face the enemy, God said, "You have too many men." God asked Gideon to reduce his fighting force to a mere three hundred men so that all would know that the victory belonged to the Lord, not to Gideon and his men (see Judges 7).

When Elijah stood alone against 450 prophets of Baal, he asked God to win the battle so the people would know that his Lord, not Baal, was the one true God (see 1 Kings 18).

God loves the weak, because in our weakness He is strong. David, Gideon, and Elijah all knew this because they experienced it firsthand. So don't be afraid to show your weakness. Your amazing God will meet you at your need and give you the strength you require. As the psalmist David wrote, "God is our refuge and strength, an ever-present help in trouble" (Psalm 46:1).

The apostle Paul writes: "I know what it is to be in need, and I know what it is to have plenty. I have learned the secret of being content in any and every situation, whether well fed or hungry, whether living in plenty or in want. I can do all this through him who gives me strength" (Philippians 4:12–13).

Jesus says: "Come to me, all you who are weary and burdened, and I will give you rest. Take my yoke upon you and learn from me, for I am gentle and humble in heart, and you will find rest for your souls. For my yoke is easy and my burden is light" (Matthew 11:28–30).

CHAPTER 41

....

GOD'S WILL FOR YOUR LIFE

*In many cases, our need to wonder about or be told
what God wants in a certain situation is nothing short of a
clear indication of how little we are engaged in His work.*
DALLAS WILLARD

You've been playing guessing games your entire life. It
began in your infancy, when your parents pestered you
with that annoying "peek-a-boo" game. As a toddler,
you were humiliated with the "guess which hand is
holding the candy" game. When you were an adolescent,
you suffered the indignity of searching for your older
siblings in a game of "hide-and-seek," only to learn
that they ditched you while you were counting to one
hundred. Now you are much older, but the guessing
games continue with picking stocks on the NASDAQ
and trying to find socks that aren't in the dryer.

As a Christian, you might be wondering if God is playing hiding games with His will for your life.

Here's the good news. This almighty God of the cosmos cares about the course and trajectory of your life. You haven't fallen off His radar. The hole in the ozone layer hasn't distracted Him from His focused interest in your life. The fact that God has a specific will for your life is obvious from verses like these:

- "Teach me to do your will, for you are my God" (Psalm 143:10).
- "Therefore do not be foolish, but understand what the Lord's will is" (Ephesians 5:17).
- "We continually ask God to fill you with the knowledge of his will" (Colossians 1:9).

But if God has a will for each believer's life, why do so many Christians have such a difficult time finding it? Maybe because they and God have different ideas of what His will looks like. God's will could take one of three forms:

- *God's Sovereign Plan*: Before God created the world, He planned exactly how things were going to go. It was more than just knowing in advance how random events were going to turn out. God is in control, and all events operate within the context of His exact plan. But for the most part, God's sovereign plan is hidden and unknown to us. The Bible tells us a little bit about a few future events, but He has told us just enough to assure us that He is in charge. God doesn't expect us to understand—or even discover—what He hasn't disclosed about His sovereign plan.

- *God's Moral Code*: God has established a moral code for all of humanity. It is simply His standard of behavior and conduct, which He has set forth in the Bible. God isn't really into rules and regulations, but He has given us beneficial principles for living. God expects faithful obedience (although He knows it won't be perfect) to these principles on our part as followers of Christ. Although these principles might be contrary to cultural preferences, we can be assured that God has our best interests in mind.

- *God's General Will for Your Life*: Before we give you the big reveal, we want to remind you of three themes that are clear in Scripture: (1) God wants you to believe in Jesus and accept Him as your Savior (see John 3:16; 2 Peter 3:9), (2) God wants you to be like Jesus (see 1 John 2:6), and (3) God wants you to know Him better and to submit to Him (see Colossians 1:9–10; Micah 6:8). Within those parameters, we can boldly and confidently pronounce God's will for your life: *it is His will for that you have a growing relationship with Him that makes you more like Christ each day.*

Were you expecting a little more personal specificity?

We'll get to that. But don't blow past God's amazing intention for you: He wants a personal relationship with you, and He wants you to be engaged in the process of becoming more Christlike. It is as simple as that. That is God's will for you.

At its core, God's will is not about a *place* or a *thing* or a *time*. God's will is all about the condition of your heart. We overlook that fact when we trivialize God's will by thinking that it primarily applies to making choices between job offers, or vacation locales, or breakfast cereals. But don't get hung up on seeking divine direction between the chocolate éclair or the yogurt parfait. God's will is more about:

- Your character than about making choices;
- Your attitude than about finding answers; and
- Your relationship with Him than about getting results.

Try to comprehend the freedom God has given you—and the confidence He has in your decision-making ability when you live in close fellowship with Him. He is not a power-hungry celestial tyrant who dictates every move that you make. He leaves many decisions to you.

The freedom God gives us to make any choice within the bounds of His moral code is consistent with God's roles characterized in Scripture—such as our King, our Father, and our Shepherd. Considering those analogies, it is natural to expect that God would have given us some decision-making freedom. That's an amazing delegation of freedom by the almighty God.

CHAPTER 42

....

GOD ANSWERS THE QUESTION
OF SUFFERING AND PAIN

God is a God of great generosity and great mercy.
He's not closing the curtain on suffering so there is more
time to gather more people into the fold of Christ's fellowship.
JONI EARECKSON TADA

This book has focused exclusively on those amazing aspects of God, which to this point includes all of them. Admittedly, we are prejudiced in favor of God, and we've made no effort to hide our bias. In fact, we even put our thesis on the cover: *God Is Amazing*. Anyone who disagrees probably wouldn't pick up this book, and if you're still reading, we can only assume that you pretty much agree with what we have written—and, more importantly, with what the Bible teaches.

At the same time, you may have had some

doubts along the way, not because you don't believe the Christian story is true but because you haven't personally experienced in your heart what you believe in your head. For example, you can talk about how amazing God's grace and mercy are, but if you perceive that God is penalizing you more than blessing you, you may not be personally experiencing these aspects of God's character. Or more likely, when you see suffering in the world, you may have reason to question the love of God. You may be asking, "Why would a loving God allow such suffering and evil?" Because the answers don't come easily, you may have serious doubts about God. Maybe He is amazing to some people, but your experience and perceptions sometimes say otherwise.

The presence of suffering and evil in the world challenges our amazing God on several of His characteristics, prompting people to ask questions like these:

- If God is *all-powerful,* why isn't He *able* to stop suffering and evil?
- If God is *all-knowing,* why doesn't He *know how* to stop suffering and evil?
- If God is *all-good,* why doesn't He *want* to stop suffering and evil?

Since suffering and evil are present in our world, the argument goes, the only conclusion many people come to is that God is not really all-powerful, all-knowing, and all-good. Therefore, the God described in the Bible isn't amazing at all. In fact, if He exists at all, He's quite ordinary.

The quick answer to these objections is actually quite simple. Just because God hasn't eliminated suffering and evil doesn't mean He is incapable, ignorant, or unwilling. From a human perspective, not doing something others think you should doesn't mean you can't, or don't know how, or don't want to. It may just mean you aren't ready to do it *right now.*

Is it possible the same logic applies to God? The apostle Peter thought so, and that's what he told the Christians in the first-century church, who were experiencing all kinds of evil and suffering because they believed in Jesus. Peter wrote, "The Lord is not slow in keeping his promise, as some understand slowness. Instead he is patient with you, not wanting anyone to perish, but everyone to come to repentance" (2 Peter 3:9).

According to Peter, the reason God isn't dealing with suffering and evil *right now* is because He is being patient with us. Because He is all-knowing, all-powerful, and all-good, God will someday defeat suffering and evil. But He's not done it yet for one simple reason: He is being patient with us because He loves us so much.

People who wish that God would deal with suffering and evil now don't realize that in order to do that, He would need to deal with those who cause the suffering and do the evil in the first place. And that's not just taking out the "bad guys," such as child-molesters, rapists, and terrorists. According to the standards of our all-holy God, we are *all* sinners who deserve to be "taken out." But in His great mercy and patience, God is holding back His final judgment until more people have time to believe in Jesus and be forgiven of their sins. You could say that our world is enjoying the benefits of God's patience, even though it means we have to endure suffering and evil for a while longer. Now *that's* amazing.

In the meantime, is there any good that can come out of suffering and evil? We believe there is—and it's a good you see every day, if not in your own circumstances then in the circumstances of others. No doubt you can think of some amazing things that have happened in the wake of a natural disaster or a tragic event. There's a resiliency and a heart of grace and forgiveness in the human spirit when we are confronted with pain that is difficult to explain apart from God. Why is this? We think it's because our amazing God knows what it's like to suffer. When He sent Jesus to take on human flesh, He knowingly sent Him to experience incredible suffering and evil. And He did it so that someday there would be an end to our own earthly woes.

Trust God in this. As much as it depends on you, do all you can to alleviate suffering and stop evil. But also be patient for the same reason God is being patient: there are more people who need to follow Him.

CHAPTER 43

....

GOD WANTS YOU TO FIND HIM IN YOUR WORLD

*If you saw a burning bush, would you
(a) call 911, (b) get the hot dogs, or (c) recognize God?*
MARY DORIA RUSSELL

Most of the time, our God-consciousness is prompted when we are in some religious kind of setting. We expect to sense the presence of God when we're in a church sanctuary, and we aren't disappointed.

But God doesn't restrict His presence to the places that are obviously religious. In fact, He is often more active in places where we might not expect to find Him. As followers of Christ, we need to be looking for the surprising places where God can be found so we can join Him in the amazing things He is accomplishing.

During the times of Abraham and Moses, it was

common for people to believe that God maintained geographic boundaries. They thought He would stay in one region and not venture forth into an enemy's turf. And even within His own region, people believed that God would show up in a temple, in an altar, or near some religious artifact. But God didn't operate that way then, and He doesn't do so now.

The Bible gives examples of God showing up at places we wouldn't expect. One of the first such accounts is found in Genesis 28. Jacob, the grandson of Abraham, had just swindled the birthright from his brother, Esau. Jacob was making a quick getaway before Esau discovered the con. By the end of the first day after his deception, he was out in the middle of nowhere, and he camped for the night. Here is the biblical description: "When he reached a certain place, he stopped for the night because the sun had set. Taking one of the stones there, he put it under his head and lay down to sleep" (Genesis 28:11).

Notice that the location is given no distinction other than it was "a certain place." That reference was a Hebrew way of saying that the spot was desolate, boring, and mundane—so obscure that it didn't even deserve a name. But it was at that spot, on that night, that Jacob had a dream in which he ascended a ladder from earth to heaven, where he encountered God, who promised protection and blessings on Jacob.

When Jacob awoke up the next morning, he expressed astonishment. It wasn't because he had encountered God—that was a common occurrence for his grandfather—rather, he was dumbfounded because God was present at that dreary desert place:

*When Jacob awoke from his sleep, he thought,
"Surely the LORD is in this place, and I was
not aware of it." He was afraid and said,
"How awesome is this place! This is none other
than the house of God; this is the gate of heaven."*
GENESIS 28:16–17

The lesson for us in this account is that God's presence is not confined to church-type settings. He can be found in places that are seemingly secular and absent of any divine signs.

There is another, perhaps more famous, story that illustrates the same principle. In the beginning chapters of Exodus, we are introduced to Moses, who, through God's intervention, was raised as the son of Egypt's Pharaoh even though he was a Jew. As a young man, he witnessed an Egyptian taskmaster cruelly abusing a fellow Jew, and he overreacted and killed the Egyptian. To avoid being executed by Pharaoh, Moses escaped to the wilderness, where he worked as a shepherd for his father-in-law for several decades. On a routine day, as he walked through the dirt and thorns in no-man's land, he saw a miraculous sight:

*The LORD appeared to him in flames of fire from
within a bush. Moses saw that though the bush was
on fire it did not burn up. So Moses thought, "I will go
over and see this strange sight—why the bush does not
burn up." . . . "Do not come any closer,"
God said. "Take off your sandals, for the place
where you are standing is holy ground."*
EXODUS 3:2–3, 5

These passages reveal a flaw in our usual expectations because we expect to find God in religious places, and we often ignore the possibility that He may reside in places and circumstances we consider routine and ordinary. But that is the surprising thing about God. He is at work all around us, and He often chooses to make the ordinary extraordinary.

The practical implication is that every place is sacred with God—because He is everywhere. So, yes, while you can expect His presence in the church building, don't overlook His presence in the boardroom, in the classroom, or in the living room. He may be expecting that you will recognize that you are on "sacred ground" when you are in your office cubicle, on the soccer practice field, or at the ATM.

Are you going to see a ladder to heaven or a shrub on fire? It's possible, but not likely. It is more probable that you will sense His presence and see a person in need. It may happen in Starbucks, where you strike up a polite conversation with an acquaintance who happens to be in trouble and needing help. Maybe you will be uncharacteristically compelled to pull off the highway to help someone whose car is broken down. Perhaps the person next to you in line at the grocery store checkout station could use a word of encouragement. The places and circumstances will all be different. The only things they have in common will be that they aren't in church-type settings—and that God is working to get your attention and move you to action.

If you are watching for burning bushes, you'll be amazed at where you find God at work.

Chapter 44

....

God Wants to Help You
Be a Better Person

In essentials, unity; in differences, liberty;
in all things, charity.
Philipp Melanchthon

Is it possible to be good without God? you ask. Well, that depends. If you're asking, "Is it possible to be good even if you don't believe God exists?" then the answer is yes. God has blessed our world with something called "common grace," which is summarized in Jesus' statement in reference to His Father: "He causes his sun to rise on the evil and the good, and sends rain on the righteous and the unrighteous" (Matthew 5:45). The love and grace of God, along with the blessings and benefits of the world He created, are for all to enjoy.

Furthermore, the good people express when they work for the betterment of the world and everyone living in it is also part of God's common grace.

By comparison, if by "good without God" you mean, "Is it possible to do good even if God doesn't exist?" well, that's a different question that deserves a different answer. Atheists are convinced we don't need God to do good. In fact, they've launched a "Good Without God" campaign by putting the phrase on buses and billboards. Their intention is to tell people they don't need God to do good things. But we would propose, as have many theologians and philosophers, that this desire to do good actually points to God.

In his book *Mere Christianity*, C.S. Lewis argued that this inner desire to do good is actually a moral obligation. It's innate, like instinct in an animal, so ingrained in our being that when we do wrong, we know it's not right. Lewis called this innate sense an "objective moral law" and held that it's not subject to conditions or circumstances. We are able to differentiate between good and bad in all circumstances, even when we don't behave like we do.

Lewis contended that an objective moral law requires an objective moral lawgiver who must be absolutely good. Otherwise all moral effort would be futile in the long run. But moral effort is not futile. Despite the evil deeds of bad guys, there are enough morally good people doing enough morally good things to keep our world inhabitable and our society civil.

Maybe this is why all religions and major belief systems in the world—except for one—are based on the concept of doing good. Even atheism, which in itself is a belief system, operates this way. Consider this atheist-sponsored slogan seen on a billboard: Doing Good Is My Religion.

The one exception to this requirement of good works is Christianity, which is based on the premise that all people fall short of God's perfect standard, and only those who put their trust in Jesus—the only person who ever lived a perfect life and did nothing but good—can make it to heaven. Of course, this contrarian belief system has led to a lot of spiritual laziness and self-centeredness. Unfortunately, there are people who view faith in Jesus as a kind of "get out of hell free" card. Once they have it, they're good to go, and it doesn't really matter how much good (or bad) they do. They've got their fire insurance policy, and it's irrevocable.

God begs to differ. First of all, people who live like that are just fooling themselves, not God (see Hebrews 10:26–27). Second, God has told us explicitly and repeatedly in His Word that He desires for us to do good. Here are just a few references:

- "For we are God's handiwork, created in Christ Jesus to do good works, which God prepared in advance for us to do" (Ephesians 2:10).
- "Let us not become weary in doing good, for at the proper time we will reap a harvest if we

do not give up" (Galatians 6:9).

- "In the same way, faith by itself, if it is not accompanied by action, is dead" (James 2:17).

There's no question about it: God wants you to do good. He wants you to be a better person. And here is the amazing part: He wants to help you do good by giving you an inside Source so you don't have to do it on your own. That Source is the Holy Spirit, who dwells in you for the purpose of helping you display those Godlike characteristics—called the fruit of the Spirit—that will help you be a better person: "But the fruit of the Spirit is love, joy, peace, forbearance, kindness, goodness, faithfulness, gentleness and self-control" (Galatians 5:22–23).

God doesn't just expect you to be a better person. He wants to help you. Now that's an amazing offer you can't refuse.

CHAPTER 45

....

GOD HAS GIVEN YOU AN ASSIGNMENT—AND THE POWER TO DO IT

The fullness of the Spirit is not a question of our getting more of the Holy Spirit, but rather of the Holy Spirit getting more of us.
OSWALD J. SMITH

After the Resurrection, Jesus gave His disciples a pep talk before He ascended to heaven. These final words, known as "the Great Commission," constitute God's assignment, which applies to all followers of Christ. Different authors have repeated it, but here is a paraphrase of the mission with which the all disciples (then and now) are tasked:

> *As you go on your way through life, teach the*

gospel message that Christ has risen from dead
and offers forgiveness of sins. Make disciples
of Christ, baptizing them, and teaching
them to observe all that Christ commanded.
(SEE MATTHEW 28:18–20 AND MARK 16:15–16)

This is amazing. As followers of Christ, our mission is to take His message and to deliver it in the manner of Christ. The God Almighty of the universe is entrusting us to be His ambassadors and His messengers.

And this is intimidating! When Christ issued this assignment, He didn't restrict its application to the religious elite. He gave it to a bunch of goofball disciples who had proven themselves to be occasionally dense to spiritual matters. They had no formal religious training, but they had spent time with Christ. And twenty centuries later, most of us are no different. We feel incapable and inadequate for the challenge. We think we don't have what it takes to accomplish what Christ instructed. But we are wrong. We *do* have what it takes, because God has amazingly given us a supernatural power source.

The evening before He was crucified, Jesus told the disciples that they would perform greater works than He had done (see John 14:12). The disciples must have been skeptical. Later that evening, and in the days before the Ascension, Jesus gave the disciples brief clues about how God would empower them to carry on what Christ had begun:

• *God will send His spirit to indwell Christ-*

followers: "And I will ask the Father, and he will give you another advocate to help you and be with you forever—the Spirit of truth" (John 14:16–17).

- *This Holy Spirit will help convict people of the need of a Savior:* "But very truly I tell you, it is for your good that I am going away. Unless I go away, the Advocate will not come to you; but if I go, I will send him to you. When he comes, he will prove the world to be in the wrong about sin and righteousness and judgment: about sin, because people do not believe in me; about righteousness, because I am going to the Father, where you can see me no longer; and about judgment, because the prince of this world now stands condemned" (John 16:7–11).

- *The Holy Spirit will bestow His power on Christians to enable them to fulfill the Great Commission:* "But you will receive power when the Holy Spirit comes on you; and you will be my witnesses in Jerusalem, and in all Judea and Samaria, and to the ends of the earth" (Acts 1:8).

And there is much more about the Holy Spirit that those first disciples learned after they received the Spirit. As the New Testament epistles explain, the Holy Spirit brings into us the character of Christ. There's a twofold benefit to us. First, we are filled with the Spirit of Christ which instills "love, joy, peace, forbearance, kindness, goodness, faithfulness, gentleness and self-control" (Galatians 5:22–23). Second, as we release our lives to Christ, His Spirit will reveal Christ's nature through us to those with whom we engage. The Holy Spirit will do the heavy lifting. We're just the vehicles that God uses to bring His Spirit to the places where we are.

We don't have to be initiators and sustainers of God's work in the world. The Holy Spirit is already at work. He is the dynamic interactive presence of the One True Living God in His people. We don't even have to be "religious"—in fact, we shouldn't be. God doesn't want us to be a religious people; He simply wants us to live life with Christ, filled with His presence and serving for His purposes.

Because of what Christ has done for us, we should willingly do whatever He asks of us, no matter how overwhelming, daunting, and seemingly outrageous His request appears. But in His graciousness, He doesn't abandon us to tackle the Great Commission on our own—stuck with nothing but own frailties and inabilities. Instead, He supernaturally empowers and equips us for the task He has assigned us. If we follow Christ, His Holy Spirit will take us into the world to love it and serve it, and to announce the presence of the risen Jesus and the hope of the world.

Bottom line: God gives us the power to perform what He asks us to do. Amazing.

CHAPTER 46

....

GOD WANTS YOU TO LOVE EVERYBODY

You can safely assume you've created God in your own image when it turns out that God hates all the same people you do.
ANNE LAMOTT

The large woman was sitting in seat 13F on the Southwest Airlines flight from Austin, Texas, to Los Angeles. Her seat was by the window, and she was trying not to make eye contact with the passengers filing by. On Southwest there are no assigned seats. People board by pre-assigned priority, and once you get on the plane you can take any open seat. The seat next to the woman in 13F remained empty for a long time. I (Stan) should know. I was sitting in 13D, two seats over. The problem with 13E—and why it was still vacant, even though most of the passengers had boarded—was a matter of space.

For all intents and purposes, the woman in 13F was also sitting in half of 13E.

I'm embarrassed to admit this, but I sat in 13D because I thought 13E might remain vacant due to the size of the woman in 13F, giving me extra room for the long flight. Then the unexpected happened. A young hipster woman (there are lots of them in Austin) walked down the aisle, stopped next to me, and pointed to 13E. She wanted to sit there. I don't know what kind of person I expected to take the "charity" case of sitting next to the woman in 13F—a nun perhaps?—but I would not have expected this young lady with a flowing white dress and several tattoos to be the one. Yet there she was, and I suddenly felt very small, especially when she sat in 13E and immediately began to engage the woman in cheerful, respectful conversation.

I don't know if my hipster seatmate was a follower of Jesus—I was feeling too sheepish to ask—but she could easily have been, for she demonstrated the Christlike quality of showing love to a person society had no doubt marginalized. And by "society," I mean me.

I believe that when Jesus told an expert in the law that the "greatest commandment" is to love God and to love your neighbor as yourself (see Matthew 22:37–40), He was thinking of people like the woman in 13F. On that flight that day, she was my neighbor, and I didn't love her. But the young woman who sat between us did, and in doing that she was being obedient to God—whether or not she was aware of it.

Many Christ-followers don't take the commandment to love their neighbor all that seriously. Oh, we like to quote the verse, and we know the story of the Good Samaritan. But when it comes to actually *loving* people—whether it's someone lying wounded in a ditch or a passenger sitting on an airplane, or someone who holds views we despise or lives in a way we don't approve of—we can be very selective. But the truth is that God wants us to love *everybody*. Jesus didn't put any qualifiers on the "love your neighbor as yourself" command. He just wants us to love. Period.

I've thought about this quite a bit since my Southwest experience, and I've come up with some categories of people who may be especially difficult to love, at least for me. This isn't an exhaustive list, but it's a start. Feel free to add categories or examples of your own.

People you disagree with or who disagree with you. How easy it is to dislike and ignore these people—and there are plenty of them. This is why there's so much contention in the world. Disagreements breed disgust. Let's not be this way.

People in need. Perhaps you sympathize with those in need, and maybe you give to organizations that help them, but do you really love them? The apostle James defines "religion that God our Father accepts as pure and faultless" this way: "to look after orphans and widows in their distress" (James 1:27). And it's impossible to look after people if you don't love them.

Your enemies. Jesus set the bar very high when He

hung on the cross, staring at His executioners and the people who were mocking him, and said, "Father forgive them." Jesus loved His enemies, and He expects us to do the same thing.

People who have a different sexual orientation. This is a big one, especially given our current cultural climate. And it's not just a matter of "hate the sin but love the sinner." Regardless of your view on this subject, you need to show genuine love, if for no other reason than to build a bridge rather than a wall.

People who don't love or believe in God. It's easy for a Christian to dislike atheists, but it's absolutely the wrong attitude. As Rick Warren once said, the only people you are ever going to win to Christ are your friends. So make friends of everyone you can, especially those who don't know the Lord. You may be surprised at the doors you open.

Chapter 47

....

The Mystery of God

A God you understand is not God.
A God you comprehend is an idol.
St. Augustine

It's wonderful to talk about our amazing God like we've been doing. Because God has left us clues about His abilities and character in the world He created, we can stand in awe of His power and greatness. Because He wrote a Book that tells His story, we have incredible insights into the depths of His love for us. And because our amazing God became human and lived among us and revealed His purposes and plans for us, we know even more about our heavenly Father through the life, death, and resurrection of His Son.

Because we know these things, we think we know

enough about God to have Him figured out. We think we know enough to treat Him as the sum of His parts, as if we've solved the puzzle and He is the answer. If that's where all of our study takes us, we've gone too far.

When we think we have God figured out, we start to impose our desires and expectations on Him. A.W. Tozer puts it much more bluntly: We make God in our image. Consequently, we think we can explain everything He does. This is completely backward and very foolish because it leads to, as Augustine wrote, idolatry of our *idea* of God rather than our reverence for the real God. Tozer agrees: "If you can explain everything about God, it isn't really God."

The Old Testament writers knew better, and their words have great credibility because they heard God's voice directly and felt His presence physically. Here's just a sampling of their impressions:

- "And these are but the outer fringe of his works; how faint the whisper we hear of him! Who then can understand the thunder of his power?" (Job 26:14).
- "Great is the LORD and most worthy of praise; his greatness no one can fathom" (Psalm 145:3).
- "For my thoughts are not your thoughts, neither are your ways my ways," declares the LORD. "As the heavens are higher than the earth, so are my ways higher than your ways and my thoughts than your thoughts" (Isaiah 55:8–9).

These verses speak to the incomprehensibility of God. That's a big word that means "God can't be figured out." But this doesn't mean God can't be known. He wants us to know Him, as He tells the prophet Jeremiah: "Let the one who boasts boast about this: that they have the understanding to know me" (Jeremiah 9:24).

So how much can we know about God? How much are we *supposed* to know? Here's the balance: you can't know God *fully*, but you can know Him *truly*. God hasn't revealed everything about Himself, but He has revealed enough for us to truly know Him.

The New Testament writers use the word *mystery* to describe God and His ways. Everyone loves a good mystery, and so it is with God. We shouldn't be frustrated with things we can't figure out or don't yet know about Him. Rather, we should enjoy and appreciate these mysteries of God:

- The mystery of Christ (Ephesians 3:2–3)
- The mystery of Christ in you (Colossians 1:27)
- The mystery of God's will (Ephesians 1:9)
- The mystery of God's wisdom (1 Corinthians 2:7)
- The mystery of the church (Ephesians 5:32)
- The mystery of the kingdom of God (Mark 4:11)
- The mystery of the gospel (Ephesians 6:19)
- The deep mystery of our faith (1 Timothy 3:9)

As you read through these passages, try not to solve them like you would a puzzle. These mysteries are bigger than your mind. They invite reflection, not resolution. Of course, it won't always be this way. There will come a day when all of these mysteries and more will unfold before us like an infinite scroll, revealing the endless beauty and wonder of our glorious and amazing God.

Reflecting on the glory of God's love, the apostle Paul penned these immortal words:

"For now we see only a reflection as in a mirror; then we shall see face to face. Now I know in part; then I shall know fully, even as I am fully known."
1 CORINTHIANS 13:12

CHAPTER 48

....

CHRISTIANITY REALLY DOES MAKE SENSE
(WHEN YOU UNDERSTAND WHO GOD IS AND WHO YOU AREN'T)

Many of the questions we ask God can't be answered directly, not because God doesn't know the answers but because our questions don't make sense. As C.S. Lewis once pointed out, many of our questions are, from God's point of view, rather like someone asking, "Is yellow square or round?" or "How many hours are there is a mile?"
N.T. WRIGHT

If you were to invent a religion, it probably wouldn't look much like Christianity. Much of what the Bible teaches seems at odds with our natural inclinations. Christianity is almost counterintuitive. A shallow overview of Christianity raises honest questions like: *If God is in charge, why does He allow evil?* and *If God can do anything He wants, why doesn't He just forgive everyone and send us all to heaven?*

Such questions can be an obstacle for some people. The moment they think Christianity doesn't make sense, they halt their investigation of it. G.K. Chesterton, a prominent twentieth–century writer, explained it this way: "The Christian ideal has not been tried and found wanting. It has been found difficult; and left untried." For many people, the "difficulty" to which Chesterton referred is the fact that Christianity seems illogical. But it is only illogical if you have an inadequate understanding of God.

Christianity will never make sense if you view God as a spiritual being who is anemic and indifferent and indecisive. It will never make sense if you attribute to God your own human characteristics and tendencies. The Bible explains why we'll be frustrated if we try to figure out why God doesn't act in the way that makes sense to us:

> *"My thoughts are nothing like your thoughts," says the LORD. "And my ways are far beyond anything you could imagine. For just as the heavens are higher than the earth, so my ways are higher than your ways and my thoughts higher than your thoughts."*
> ISAIAH 55:8–9 NLT

But if God is viewed as He is presented in the Bible—sovereign, almighty, loving, just, and all-knowing—then the blueprint of Christianity makes sense:

- *God has always existed.* He had no beginning; He will have no end. He operates outside the dimensions of time and space.
- *God is sovereign and all-powerful.* The cosmos was created at His command, and everything in the universe operates under His purview. There is no act of nature or any circumstance in our lives that happens outside His authority.
- *God is holy.* He is not just morally good; He is perfect—which is incomprehensible to us. He is free of any evil thought or action. His holiness cannot be compromised; He cannot abide any breach of His holiness.
- *God is love.* He created humanity to live in companionship with Him. This was an act of love with the intent that humanity would respond with love toward Him. No ego or conceit was involved. He is God, so He is worthy of humanity's worship and adoration. The extent of God's love caused Him to gift us with the freedom of choice—the choice to follow Him or to reject Him.

Exercising our freewill, humanity has proven to be prideful and selfish. We desire our own way and rebel against God's precepts. This rebellion merits God's punishment. He is a just God, and any rejection, rebellion, or disobedience toward Him merits a death penalty. If that seems harsh, then we overestimate our self-importance and underestimate God's holiness. Our distorted human nature makes us minimize the gravity of our sin. To us, it may seem like "no big deal." But we need to view our sin from God's righteous perspective.

But God is also full of mercy and grace. His merciful plan can spare us from the punishment we deserve. His grace offers reconciliation that we don't deserve. God extends His forgiveness, grace, and mercy to us freely. However, they cannot be extended without the consequence of death—remember that He is a just God who requires a penalty for sin. In the ultimate act of love, God allowed His perfect Son to be crucified for our transgressions. Being sinless Himself, His death was a qualifying sacrifice sufficient to pay the penalty for our transgressions. Christ's death proved His love for us; His resurrection proved that He was God.

God extends His offer of salvation to all people. It is based completely on the sacrifice of Christ. There is no "performance" required on our part. It is just as amazing as it sounds: those who put their faith and trust in Christ are immediately restored to intimacy with the almighty God of the universe.

Like our salvation, our continuing relationship with Christ is not performance-based. Followers of Christ are not in jeopardy of being kicked out of God's family when they mess up. Of course, true Christ-followers desire to live according to God's principles, but this is a matter of voluntary submission and commitment motivated by responsive gratitude. Perfection is not required; it is not even expected. God's love, grace, and forgiveness extend to His followers with His foreknowledge that we will screw up along the way.

At some time in the future, God will restore order at the completion of His plan. Evil will be conquered permanently, and Christ-followers—from the past and present—will reign with Him for eternity in a perfect creation.

It is an amazing scenario. But it is logical, rational, and compelling—when you understand that God is amazing.

AFTERWORD

....

We hope you've enjoyed this look at our amazing God. We hope you've gained a new appreciation for God's infinite qualities, His creative power, His awesome Son, and His amazing grace. At the same time, we hope and pray your experience has gone beyond enjoyment and appreciation.

You see, you can enjoy and appreciate—even be amazed by—something without it affecting your life in any meaningful way. Think about it: a good movie or a beautiful sunset can entertain or awe us, but then we get on to something else and forget about what we've just experienced. If that's the way it's been for you while reading this book, we'd like to give you one more amazing thought: You can know God personally. You don't have to leave Him in this book, like a photo stored in your phone. You can invite the amazing God into your life simply by telling Him, right now, how far short you've fallen when measured against His amazing holiness. . .how weak you feel when compared to His amazing strength. . .how utterly amazing it is that Jesus died so you could live with God forever.

If you're not sure about this right now, that's okay. But rather than put God on a shelf like you would this book, why not give Him a try? Live for a while as if you do have a personal relationship with Him. Talk to a friend who knows God this way. Find a Bible and read about Jesus. Pray and ask God to show you His amazing love.

You might be amazed at what God will do.

About Bruce and Stan

Bruce and Stan have co-authored more than sixty books about the Christian faith, including bestsellers such as *God Is in the Small Stuff—and it all matters.* They are passionate about presenting the truth of God in a manner that is clear, casual, concise, and correct.

When Bruce Bickel didn't make the cut as a stand-up comedian, he became a lawyer, which is a career in which he's considered hilarious. He is active in church ministries and currently serves on the Board of Westmont College. He lives in Central California with his wife, where kids and grandkids surround them.

Stan Jantz has been involved with content throughout his professional career as a bookseller, publisher, and writer. He resides with his wife in Southern California, where he serves on the board of trustees of Biola University.

If you have any questions, comments, or just want to share a story about your amazing God, visit www.godisamazingbook.com or contact Bruce and Stan at info@godisamazingbook.com

Also Available from Shiloh Run Press. . .

978-1-63058-355-2
God Is Amazing Audio

Get it wherever great audiobooks are sold.